Dr. JOHN EWING

DR. JOHN EWING
AND SOME OF HIS NOTED CONNECTIONS

BY
LUCY E. LEE EWING

PHILADELPHIA
NINETEEN HUNDRED TWENTY-FOUR

COPYRIGHT 1924, BY
LUCY E. LEE EWING

PRESS OF
ALLEN, LANE & SCOTT
PHILADELPHIA

INTRODUCTION

THE real story of a real man is more interesting than any fiction, just as the actual is nearer to us than the possible. This volume written by the great-granddaughter of Dr. John Ewing, who was Provost of the University of Pennsylvania, 1779-1802, contains valuable information about him and a number of members of his family. We are fortunate indeed to have these records brought together and rendered accessible in a form so attractive in style and mode of presentation. The personal is after all what most interests us, and these descriptions of characters of distinguished people constitute a valuable contribution to our knowledge and understanding of the lives of those who preceded us. There were giants in those days, and the accounts of Provost Ewing show clearly the breadth and depth of his scholarship and the greatness of his influence upon those who were so fortunate as to know him.

To the history of education in America this volume is, likewise, a contribution, for the University of Pennsylvania, over which Provost Ewing presided, was the first institution in this country to have the title "University" and in the earlier form of its title, it was the first "State University" being the "University of the State of Pennsylvania." Merged with the College of Philadelphia, in 1791, the united institutions became the "University of Pennsylvania," a title borne ever since.

JOSIAH H. PENNIMAN,
Provost.

The University of Pennsylvania,
    March, 1924.

CHAPTER I.

DR. JOHN EWING.

THERE is something in the mingling of the Scotch with the Irish in the North of Ireland which produces intellect of a high order. The sturdy strength and Celtic wit of the Scotch, added to the lighter and perhaps greater brilliancy of the Southern Celts, makes a combination peculiar to that locality.

As pupil, scholar, Provost of the University of Pennsylvania and ranking high as a mathematician and astronomer, John Ewing was a notable example. About 1700, four Ewing brothers came from Londonderry, Ireland, and settled in Cecil County, Maryland. It was after the Battle of the Boyne, when so many families were impoverished.

Several younger brothers came over in 1718, and settled on Long Island, afterwards removing to New Jersey. The father of this numerous family was of Scotch descent and lived in Londonderry. For his distinguished bravery in the Battle of the Boyne, King William presented him with a sword which was brought by the younger brothers to America.

Of the four brothers who came to Maryland, John, the oldest, went west and from him are descended many distinguished men and women in Ohio and Kentucky.

Alexander and his brother, Henry, settled in East Nottingham, near what was afterwards called Ewingville, while Samuel established himself in West Nottingham and married Rebecca George, who came from North Wales with Quaker preachers.

Alexander was the father of five sons and several daughters, William, George, Alexander and the twins, James and John, born June 22, 1732, the same year and day of month made famous by the birth of Washington. We do not know much about the early years of John Ewing, but he seems to have loved every thing connected with books and to have overcome every obstacle in order to obtain a liberal education. The school-house was some distance from his father's residence. The little he acquired there was all that was needed to fire the ambition of such a mind. He was soon removed and placed under the superintendence of Dr. Alison, an eminent and learned clergyman, who directed a school at New London Cross Roads in Pennsylvania, and after finishing his studies John remained three years as a tutor in the school. This was almost a necessity, as his father had died and left his property to be distributed according to the laws of the State of Maryland, in which that of primogeniture prevailed. The eldest son, William, inherited the patrimonial estate, while John and his brothers received £20 each.

John Ewing had his Boswell in the Vice-Provost of the University of Pennsylvania, a very distinguished man and scholar, Robert Patterson, who had been Brigade-Major of the Revolutionary Army, Professor of Mathematics in the University, Director of the United States Mint, and Secretary, Vice-President and President of the American Philosophical Society. His beautifully written sketch of Dr. Ewing's career was published in the *Port Folio* of March, 1813, eleven years after my great-grandfather's death.

It was also included as a biographical sketch in Dr. Ewing's *Natural Philosophy*, which Mr. Patterson had arranged and published in 1809. His appreciative biographer writes:—

"Under the kind care of Dr. Alison he made considerable progress in his favourite pursuit, the study of mathematics. Books of science were not at that time easily obtained in America, especially in places remote from cities; but such was his thirst for knowledge that he frequently rode thirty or forty miles to obtain the loan of a book which might afford him some information on the subject of his favourite speculations. Those authors who were safe guides could not always be obtained. Incorrect writings sometimes fell into his hands, the errors of which did not escape the detection of his penetrating and original genius. It often occurs that difficulties only quicken the eagerness of the mind in its pursuits, and bring into action its latent energies. Such was the result of difficulties on Dr. Ewing at this early period of his life. His mind did not shrink from intellectual conflict, but gathered vigour from hindrance, and bade defiance to difficulty. At this period he certainly learned much from books, and much from the conversation of Dr. Alison, of whom indeed he always spoke with kindness, but he acquired more from the habits of close thinking in which he early indulged. To the two former he was much indebted, but if we allow to those sources of information all that they merit, it will yet not be hazardous to say that in the science of mathematics he was self-taught, and could never have reached that station which he afterwards adorned, struggling as he was with poverty and harassed with difficulties, without receiving from other than human aid the impulse which carried him forward.

"In the year 1754 he left the school of Dr. Alison, and removed to Princeton for the purpose of entering the college. Mr. Burr, the father of the late vice-president of the United States, was then president of that institution, and of that great and celebrated man he was a favourite pupil. He joined the senior class, and, impelled by pecuniary embarrassments, engaged at the same time as teacher of the grammar school which was connected with the college. His intention was to graduate, and for this purpose it was necessary that he should study in private some branches of learning to which he had previously been unable to attend. These causes made his labour greater than that of his classmates. His studies were arduous and multiplied; but he brought to the contest a mind which difficulties did not easily subdue. He graduated with his class in the year 1755, and finding that he had still to toil for a subsistence, he immediately accepted the appointment of tutor in the college. At this period he resolved to choose his profession; and feeling the study of theology congenial with his wishes, and calculated to permit him to mingle with it scientific researches, he adopted it with his usual promptitude and his usual zeal.

"In pursuance of this design, he returned to Dr. Alison, his former tutor and friend, and, after the usual period of preparatory study, he was licensed to preach the Gospel by the presbytery of Newcastle, in the state of Delaware. At the age of twenty-six, before he undertook the pastoral charge of any congregation, he was selected to instruct the philosophical classes in the college of Philadelphia, during the absence of the provost, the late Dr. William Smith. Whilst he was engaged in the discharge of this honourable office, he received an invitation from the presbyterian congregation of his native place to settle himself among them as their pastor. This was an invitation on which he deliberated, before he declined it. To be selected by the friends of his youth as their spiritual guide; to fix himself with a decent stipend on his native spot among his relations and former associates, was a temptation calculated to win a man who was social in his affections, and who was little troubled with the unquiet spirit of ambition. But he was by this time married, and having early known the value of a liberal education, he wished to give his offspring the opportunity of possessing those instructions which he himself had so long toiled to acquire; which, during his life, he praised as more valuable than wealth, and recommended to the attention of his children by all the persuasions of paternal affection. Whilst, however, he was deliberating, he received, in the year 1759, an unanimous invitation from the first presbyterian congregation in the city of Philadelphia to undertake their pastoral charge. This he did not feel himself at liberty to decline, but accepted it, and fixed himself for his life.

"From this period until the year 1773, he continued to discharge his duties with a diligence and zeal seldom surpassed. In the bosom of his congregation he found affection and friendship, and learned that life has few stations to offer to an unambitious heart more valuable than that of a pastor beloved by his flock. He was now at liberty to pursue his favourite studies without other intrusions on his time than method and diligence could render harmless. During this period his studious researches enabled him to accumulate materials for the compilation of his *Lectures on Natural Philosophy,* and such was the vigour of his understanding, such his habits of constant study, and so ample his stores of knowledge, that the volume published in 1809 is copied from the original manuscript.

"New scenes now opened upon his view. In the year 1773 he was commissioned, with the consent of his congregation, in conjunction with Dr. Hugh Williamson, late a member of congress from the state of North Carolina, to solicit subscriptions in Great Britain for the academy of Newark in the state of Delaware. He took with him letters of recommendation from men of science and respectability to several eminent characters. These, aided by his own reputation for mathematical science, his general information, and his virtues, procured for him the intimacy and friendship of several persons, who at that period and since held the highest stations of literature. Among these were the celebrated historian Dr. Robertson, Dr. Webster, Mr. Balfour, and Dr. Blacklock, the blind poet of Scotland. He visited every place of importance in England, Scotland, and Ireland, and in all of them was received with that attention and respect which are due to the man of science and the minister of God. The cities of Glasgow, Montrose, Dundee and Perth, presented to him their freedom, and, from the university of Edinburgh, of which Dr. Robertson was then the *Principal*, he received, without application, the degree of Doctor of Divinity. Dr. Robertson, on presenting his diploma, declared that he had never before conferred a degree with greater pleasure. The acquaintance, thus commenced with this celebrated personage, ripened into intimacy, and until the death of the latter, in 1793, he made constant and affectionate inquiries about Dr. Ewing from travelling Americans who visited him at Edinburgh. A few days before his death, some young American gentlemen waited upon him, to whom he spoke of his friend '*as a man of great talents for whom he entertained a great personal regard,*' and his last words at parting were, '*Do not forget to present my kind regards to Dr. Ewing.*'

"Such a testimonial from such a man as the historian of Charles the Fifth, the descendants of Dr. Ewing may be permitted to remember and to speak of to the world.

"When he first visited England, the approaching contest with his native land was a topic of conversation in every society. He was warmly and uniformly the friend of his country, and although he had frequent offers of reward from men, high in power, if he would remain in England, yet his knowledge of the causes of the revolution, his acquaintance with the spirit and resources of his countrymen, and his integrity forbade him to listen to them. He held frequent conversations with the minister, lord North, to whom, with that frankness and independence of sentiment which characterized him, he communicated all his information respecting the resources and power of the people of the united colonies. To the minister he predicted the issue of the contest, and urged him to pause before he alienated irretrievably from the mother country the affections of loyal subjects. These conversations he was in the habit of repeating to his friends on his return from England, not without some degree of surprise that the minister should have involved his country in a war with a people, of whose character, numbers, spirit and resources he was utterly ignorant.

"Among the eminent literary characters whom Dr. Ewing met at the hospitable table of Mr. Dilly, the London bookseller, was the truly great Dr. Johnson. He loved to speak to his friends of this interview, which serves to illustrate the character of a man, of whom every one, who has read, knows something. When Mr. Dilly invited Dr. Ewing to dine with him, he added, 'You will meet the great Dr. Johnson, but you must not contradict him; we never contradict him.' The day arrived, and Dr. Ewing, on entering the parlour of Mr. Dilly, found several eminent literary characters engaged in easy conversation, which, however, was instantly suspended when Dr. Johnson entered the room. There was a general silence. He scarcely noticed any one, but, seizing a book which lay on the table, read in it attentively until dinner was announced. Here, every one seemed to forget himself, and anxious to please him by the most assiduous attentions. He attended however to nothing but his plate. He did not seem to know that any one was present, until, having eaten voraciously without exhibiting many of those *graces* which constituted so great a portion of Chesterfield's morality, he raised his head slowly, and, looking around the table, surveyed the guests for the first time. They were then engaged in a discussion of the expected controversy with America, and, as Dr. Ewing had lately left his native country, he, with his usual frankness, and without adverting to, or regarding the prejudices of Dr. Johnson, began to defend the cause of the colonies. Johnson looked at him with sternness, and said, *'What do you know, Sir, on that subject?'* Mr. Dilly's caution was forgotten, and Dr. Ewing calmly replied, that having resided in America during his life, he thought himself qualified to deliver his opinions on the subject under discussion. This produced an animated conversation. Johnson's prejudices against the Americans were strong; he considered them, as he always termed them, rebels and scoundrels, and these epithets were now by no means sparingly used. It is difficult to say how far he might have been provoked, by opposition in argument, if a fortunate turn had not been given to the dispute. Johnson had rudely said, 'Sir, what do *you* know in America. You never read. You have no books there.' 'Pardon me, sir,' replied Dr. Ewing, 'we have read the *Rambler.*' This civility instantly pacified him, and, after the rest of the company had retired, he sat with Dr. Ewing until midnight, speaking amicably and eloquently, and uttering such wisdom as seldom falls from the lips of man.

"In the summer of 1775, Dr. Ewing returned to his native land, with a mind highly improved by his travels. He had directed his inquiries to the study of man, in all the varieties which Great Britain and Ireland afforded. He had collected much information and many anecdotes, which on his return were observed for the amusement and instruction of that social circle, which he loved to collect at his own fireside. His parlour was always the scene of cheerfulness and hospitality. His finances indeed were never more than moderate, but he was always able to furnish for his guests something more valuable than the delicacies of the season, or the wines of France.

"War had now commenced between the United States and Great Britain, and he adhered to the cause of his country with steadiness and zeal. When the British army was expected in Philadelphia in 1777, he removed his family to his native place, where he continued to reside until the city was evacuated by *Clinton,* immediately before his retreat through the state of Newjersey to Newyork He then returned to his congregation, and in 1779 was elected to the provostship of the university of Pennsylvania, which station he filled until his death.

"To this station he was fully competent. In all the branches of learning and science usually taught in colleges, he was uncommonly accurate, and in his mode of instruction and of communicating information he was probably never surpassed. On his appointment he prepared the Lectures which have been published, and which he delivered to his pupils during a period of twenty years. They contain all that is necessary for the mere student; written in a plain and simple style, and arranged with great method and perspicuity. As a teacher perhaps no one was ever more beloved. His authority over his pupils was that of a parent, and while he maintained that discipline without which genius will be wasted, and diligence useless, he won their affection by the mildest manners.

"All his hours were now occupied. He attended at the university during the mornings and afternoons of every day, and devoted his remaining time to the duties of his pastoral charge, and a necessary attention to his private affairs. These were arduous and multiplied. Visiting the sick, and interchanging with his parishioners the visits of friendship, occupied much of his time. And when from the performance of these duties, he retired to his closet, he was obliged to prepare, usually two, but always at least one discourse for the approaching sabbath. But these difficulties yielded to his love of method and untiring diligence. He rose with the sun, and retired to rest at a late hour in the night; yet his constitution was naturally so robust, and the care of his health so judicious, that, during a period of forty years, he was never prevented by sickness from attending to his pastoral duties.

"But these were not his only employments. His mathematical reputation attracted the attention of his fellow citizens, and on various occasions he was appointed to perform public duties. He was one of those gentlemen who were commissioned to run the boundary line of the state of Delaware, and to settle the boundary line between the states of Massachusetts and Connecticut and between Pennsylvania and Virginia. He was also appointed in conjunction with the late David Rittenhouse, by the state of Pennsylvania, to survey the most practicable ground for a turnpike road between Philadelphia and Lancaster. He was a distinguished member, and for some time one of the vice-presidents of the American Philosophical Society, to which he made several valuable communications, which are recorded in the volumes of their transactions.* He also made

---

* The following were the communications which he made to the A. P. S. "An account of the Transit of Venus over the sun, June 3d, 1769, and of the Transit of Mercury, November 9th, 1769, both as observed

several valuable additions to the astronomical articles in the American edition of the British Encyclopædia, published by Mr. Thomas Dobson. About the year 1795, he commenced the compilation of a course of Lectures on Natural History, for the use of the pupils in the university, and made some progress in the work, but his health did not permit him to complete his plan.

"From the year 1779 to the time of his death, his life had little variety. He continued to discharge the various duties of pastor, preceptor, husband, parent, and friend, without making, as it is believed, one good man his foe. The compensation which he received from the university and from the church, although not large, enabled him, with economy, to raise a numerous family, and to acquire a moderate property. But he was not versed in the artifices of business. He was a friend, and he trusted. He was himself free from guile, and therefore easily duped, and thus, in his old age, he had the mortification to see his little property swept from him by those to whom he had formerly loved to render acts of kindness. Yet he did not speak harshly of those who had injured him. Some of them indeed he forgave, though he could not forget. But for the conduct of the rest, he was always desirous to find excuses, and he continued during his life to defend those who could find no other apologist.

"In the summer of 1796 he was attacked with a violent disorder, which it required a long time to subdue. He never however recovered from its effects; but although it left him so feeble as to be unable to walk without aid, he still persevered in performing his public duties. His remaining strength began to fail him during the early part of the year 1802, and in the month of August, he removed

---

in the statehouse, Philadelphia." "An improvement in the construction of Godfrey's Quadrant."

his family on account of the yellow fever to the house of his son in Montgomery county, in Pennsylvania, where he died on the 8th of September of that year, in the 71st year of his age.

"The following sketch is extracted from a funeral sermon preached by his pastoral successor, the rev. Dr. John Blair Linn, on the 21st of November, 1802, in the first Presbyterian Church, in the city of Philadelphia.

" 'The unembellished incidents which have now been narrated of Dr. Ewing's life, his religious and scientifical writings; his observations and deportment in the different relations of society, declare that his mind was uncommonly strong and penetrating, and that he had a mild and correct taste. Were we to distinguish between his powers, we would say that his understanding predominated over his imagination. He had more the mind of Locke than of Milton. He looked through nature more with the eye of the philosopher than of the poet. The sublimer and minuter forms of matter were objects of his investigation; and we cannot but suppose him to have been gifted with diversified talents, who could scan the illuminated glories of the heavens, and inspect the insect which is only visible to the microscopic eye: We cannot but suppose that his researches were extensive, who looked into the mind of man, analyzed his faculties and affections; who unfolded to him the great truths of his God, who looked through the howling wilds and taught the properties of the brutal tribes, who looked through the fields of air and described the race which travel on the wing. In the science of mathematics, Dr. Ewing, if not unrivalled, was unsurpassed by any character in this country. His knowledge of the learned languages was very considerable. The Hebrew language, which is too often neglected by the ministers of God in the present day, was one of his favourite studies. In the mornings of his latter days, he always read a portion of the scriptures in their original tongue; and you could seldom enter his room without seeing on his couch beside him his Hebrew bible. His qualifications as a minister of the gospel were many and eminent. Science was to him a powerful assistant in the labours of his sacred office. She was with him a handmaid to religion, and, aided by her, he was an able champion of the cross, both in the advocation of its cause and in the repulsion of the attacks of impiety and error. He was mighty in the scriptures. To the fountain of all religious knowledge he went for instruction. His religious opinions were not so much founded upon the systems written by fallible men, as upon the scriptures of infallibility. He adopted not Calvin or Arminius, or Socinus, but the word of God as his guide. He read, he examined, he decided for himself. With the works of commentators and systematical writers he was familiar; he considered them as indispensable assistants to the student, but his veneration for these did not impress upon him a blind obedience to their dictates: He was first convinced by his own researches that they corresponded with the sacred volume, before he acknowledged their authority. His own investigation confirmed him in his belief of the doctrines of grace. These were the doctrines which he preached and which he endeavored to impress upon the hearts of his people.* His discourses were written with accuracy; the truths which they contained were well examined and digested before he ventured to offer them to the public. He thought it a duty which he owed to his God and his hearers, to think before he spoke, to study and to ponder in private, before he arose

---

* "Among the practical writers he thought that Doddridge was the best: and he thought that the method which he followed in his discourses was a good model for the practical and devout preacher."

in the presence of an audience as the messenger from heaven. To God he looked for aid and support; but he looked for assistance in his study, before he trusted to divine impulse in the sacred desk. Perhaps it may be said with truth that no minister in this country has adopted a better method of instruction than that which distinguished his discourses; and perhaps it may be said that none more fully illustrated and confirmed by plain and decisive reasoning, the passage which he chose for discussion. The style in which he embodied his conceptions was always perspicuous and occasionally ornamental. Ornament however he did not often employ. He sometimes poured forth "thoughts that breathed and words that burned," but his most usual manner was sober and temperate, such as was adopted before him by Tillotson and Sherlock. Mere declamation was never heard from him; his discourses were always solid and edifying, and so equal in the scale of merit; that perhaps to no one which he wrote in the vigour of his mind could a decided preference be given.'

" 'His delivery was pleasing and happy. If, in his old age, from debility, it was not remarkable for animation, yet it was distinguished for correctness, and could sometimes touch the finest springs of tenderness and pity.

" 'The temper of Dr. Ewing was generous, and not often ruffled. His manners and deportment were easy and affable. Free from guile himself, he suspected not guile in others. He had a freeness of salutation which sometimes surprised the stranger, but which was admired by those who knew him, as it proceeded from a heart open and honest. His talents for conversation were remarkably entertaining. From severer studies he could unbend, and become the companion of innocent mirth and happy gayety. In the house of bidden joy his religion did not wear the frown; it covered not itself with the mantle of sorrow, but it taught him to rejoice with those that rejoice, as well as to weep with those that weep. He was perfectly free from pedantry, and from every thing that bore its resemblance. In the company of philosophers, he was in his conversation the philosopher, and with the unlettered, the man of ease and accommodation. His talent of narration was universally admired. His observation of men and manners in this country and abroad furnished him with many scenes and facts which as painted and related by him were extremely entertaining. In domestic life he was amiable. He had all the heart of the husband; he had all the heart of the parent; he had the full heart of a friend; surrounded by a large family, he had care and tenderness for them all. His affection for his children was such that, even in his moments of severest study, he received them with smiles, and laid aside his books to partake of their infantile sports.

" 'Dr. Ewing was tall in his person, and, while in younger life, was handsome and graceful. His constitution was remarkably sound and strong. He was settled with his congregation forty years without being prevented more than once or twice by sickness from discharging the duty of his pastoral charge. The only serious disorder which he had, was the one which proved fatal, and which first seized him (in 1796) six years before his death. After his first attack he frequently preached, but never regained his strength of body, or vigour of mind. In his sickness he discovered patience, fortitude and resignation to the will of his heavenly Father. No murmur escaped his lips, and his last moments were closed apparently without a pang and without a struggle. In a good old age, in his seventy-first year, he fell to the ground *like as a shock of corn cometh in his season.* A short time before his death he buried the last of those members of his congregation who signed his call.' "

CHAPTER II.

THE SERGEANTS.

HANNAH SERGEANT, who married John Ewing was a daughter of Jonathan Sergeant. There were five or six Jonathan Sergeants back of him and the third founded Newark.

Hannah's mother was Hannah Dod of Newark and her mother, Hannah Witman of Edinburgh.

Jonathan Dickinson Sergeant was the son of Jonathan, by his second wife, Abigail Dickinson and it was to this brother-in-law, John Ewing entrusted his affairs during his absence in Great Britain. A few years ago the Woman's Dormitory of the University was named the Hannah Sergeant Hall after his wife and her portrait adorns the Hall and is an exact copy of the miniature, which is in the possession of the writer, her great-granddaughter.

The following letters were written to Hannah when her husband was travelling in Great Britain, getting aid for a college in Newark. It was about the time of the Boston Tea Party and the letters give an interesting account of the trend of events in that momentous period of our history and the diversity of opinion among the British, and how the politics of the day annoyed Dr. Ewing and interfered with his mission for the college.

The letters were discovered by his great-granddaughter between the pages of a tattered magazine where they had been placed by some unknown hand a hundred and more years ago. That they fell into the possession of his daughter, Mrs. Sarah Hall and were by her sent to her son,

JONATHAN DICKINSON SERGEANT

John Elihu Hall, at that time editor of the *Port Folio* in Philadelphia, is made plain by the following letter accompanying them:—

"JUNE 9th.

"MY DEAR JACK:—

"Having so good an opportunity I venture to send you your grandfather's letters. You will be careful of them for they are a treasure to me. There were many more but they are scattered about in the family. You will find with them some letters of Dr. Williamson who was with him. I suppose you know him as he is an author, member of Congress, etc. Their business was to collect money for the Newark Academy. Dr. W. had been to the West Indies before this European tour for the same purpose.

"You will see some lady letters too and find that they write as American ladies are wont to do. One of them is, we suppose from circumstances, Mrs. Grant's friend, Isabella Ewing.

"The letters are rather domestic than descriptive and perhaps will disappoint you. Let me know at any rate how you like them. Take *great care* of them and bring them back to me.

"Your affectionate mother,

"S. H."

First Letter.

"LONDON, Feb. 20th, 1774.

"MY DEAR:—

"I wrote you about the beginning of this month by the way of New York.

"I think it was by Campbell, but I am told that it is likely that this may reach you as soon as that, so that I might have delayed writing till this opportunity had it not have been, that I am desirous of improving every one that offers; which I hope you will also do.

"However, I am in company every day, yet I have not the same satisfaction that I would have from being with you and children. Although I much desire to be at home again, yet I must stay here until I have completed my business which I yet hope to accomplish in ye time I have proposed.

"Many difficulties arise in ye course of our business. The destruction of ye Tea at Boston and ye sending it back from Phil'a greatly retards our progress. We are almost accounted Rebels here and many say that they will not give money to those who refuse to submit to ye Parliament of Great Britain.

"Dr. Witherspoon has also wrote against, alleging that our Academy will hurt the Jersey College and that it is intended to teach other doctrines in Divinity than what are taught in his College. Although this will hurt us, yet it will not defeat our mission.

"The selfishness and contracted spirit which he has hereby manifested has raised a contempt for him in the breasts of some who before thought well of him.

"The news of his letter has just arrived in town and at first hearing sundry gentlemen have told me we ought to be supported against such an attempt to hinder the progress of religion and learning among us. I hope Jonathan will see him concerning this matter and report it in a spirited manner; yet I would not have him hurt himself on my account.

"I have sent you a pack of optical cards for ye children to learn something of that science by ye proper directions for the use of them are contained in ye little book, sealed up with them. Tell them they must not soil them nor read or play with them, but when they have washed their hands. They were invented by a Baptist clergyman here who presented them to me.

"Let the children be kept constantly at school. I think that Polly should go longer, as we shall be able to give them little or no fortune they should have as good learning as we can give them. I hope Billy keeps close to his ciphering and that he takes so much delight in it as to make progress. The girls should also learn something of figures.

"I have got your picture set in the lid of my snuff box and consequently see it ten times in a day, and sometimes in an hour. Tell Miss Polly that it is not as pretty as the original. I must have her to mend it when I return. I could have sent you a case for mine, but expect that you have got it set by this time and that you wear it daily.

"I would have sent you a pair of bracelets to wear on your arms, but that you would not wear them as not being fashionable in Phil'a. If you think of anything that would be agreeable to you or ye children mention it and I will send it by the first conveyance.

"I am, my dear,
   "Yours etc.,
"LONDON.   "JOHN EWING."

Second Letter.

"LONDON, April 18th, 1774.
"By Mrs. Williams.

"MY DEAR:—

"I received yours of ye 9th of February a few days ago, which after three months of silence from America was very satisfactory. I am surprised that all that time you had not heard of my arrival, as I wrote by the Packet on ye first of December and frequently since that time. Upon the whole I have been very well since I came here, allowance being made for my absence from home and ye. Difficulties of my mission, which makes me low spirited sometimes.

"You talk of parting with David which I am satisfied with. If you do, let me know that I may bring over a boy with me when I come.

"I think you had better send Billy to Newark as soon as you can. If I remember well, I mentioned it in one of my former letters. It is time for him to be there. I suppose he has made good progress in his ciphering and writing. Dr. Allison will tell you what books to get for him.

"I have bought a very fine Bible for Miss Sallie King, it is of the best kind and very neatly bound. I hope she will like it. If she does not keep it, as I esteem it very much on account of ye notes. The books for Mrs. Heckey are also bought and will be sent on the vessel that brings this, together with a copy of ye *Spectator* for ye girls. I set out this week for Edinburgh to meet the General Assembly. From thence I propose to go over to Ireland and return to England at ye end of August. The remainder of the summer I shall spend in England, going through ye various towns, where I have any prospect of success, leaving no stone unturned to accomplish my business which will take more time than either you or I imagined at first. We are obliged to let ye storm against America blow over in some measure, before we can do much. The Parliament seem determined to reduce ye Colonies to obedience (torn off)
has already passed to shut up ye Port of Boston until they pay for ye tea and give security to pay all duties.

"Lord North has brought in two Bills more, one to alter their Charter in various particulars and another to prevent any persons being tried in the Province who may kill any of ye inhabitants in endeavoring to enforce ye laws or collect ye duties and to authorize ye Government to send them with the witnesses to England for their trial. Having wrote to you lately by the way of Baltimore and New York I have nothing further to say at this time than to give compliments to all friends. I heartily sympathize with Mrs. Johnson in ye loss of her husband. Present her my compliments of condolence. With love to ye children, I am,

"Yrs,

"JOHN EWING."

Third Letter.

"LONDON, 1774.

"MY DEAR:—

"As the last accounts from Phil'a from Mr. Sam'l Caldwell informed me of a slight fit of sickness you had, as he called it of which you were not then recovered; I have been very uneasy ever since and I must continue so until I hear from you. This should make you careful to write me every month. You can easily convey a letter to New York to come by the Packet when there are no vessels for London at Phil'a. I would not, I never did suspect a want of affection. Uneasyness however cannot be avoided if I do not hear from you frequently.

"To be four months without any intelligence from Home is too long a time. I have not heard whether you know that I arrived here, altho' I have wrote often to you, and have scarcely suffered a single opportunity to escape.

"As I shall set out for Edinburgh next week to meet ye Gen'l Assembly of the Church of Scotland you cannot expect to hear from me as often as you would was I to continue here. I find my health considerable improved and particularly by a journey I took lately to Bath to wait on Lady Huntington for her countenance and assistance in our business. She by the way has not only promised me a subscription, but also some letters to her friends which I expect will be of great advantage.

"Dr. Williamson has cast his eyes upon a pretty widow in town with fine eyes and about as tall as yourself she is well bred, sensible and sprightly, with two sons and an old mother about 70 years of age. After saying so much need I mention that she has about six thousand Pounds Sterling and is 29 years of age. Each of her children has as good a fortune left by their Father in the Hands of Executors who have ye sole Direction of their Education and consequently will not permit them to be under her management, if she should marry. It is no small sacrifice for her to give up her native Country and her mother and children and go with him to America. However, I believe she will do so. The matter is almost concluded. Upon saying this to the Doctor, he replied that it was more than *almost concluded* and my next will give you account of its accomplishment. I need not trouble you with Politics as I said enough on this subject in a letter I sent you lately.

"Nothing material has happened since. Ask Jonathan if he would care to be made a member of ye Governors Council in the Jerseys, if I could procure him a Commission for it, which I believe I can do thro' my acquaintance with Lord Dartmouth. Do not mention this to any person but himself and let him write me per next Packet. If he likes ye thing I will try to accomplish it for him.

"I am yours etc.,
"JOHN EWING."

THE EWING AND SERGEANT COAT OF ARMS COMBINED
(Made in England)

Fourth Letter.

"Glasgow, May 3rd, 1775.

"My Dear:—

"I have been at my old Friend's Mrs. Ewing's this ten days, waiting for the meeting of the Presbytery of Glasgow.

"They met yesterday and advise a further delay of a collection here until the public affairs are settled, when they expect that something considerable may be obtained in this and the neighboring towns. I wrote you about two weeks ago by Mr. William Miller's nephew whom I saw accidentally at Greenwich as he was going on Board for Phil'a. He told me that he had a letter for me from Dr. Webster which he promised to send on shore, but he did not. I suppose he had no opportunity. Keep it safe for me till I come, which I hope will be soon now. I have gone over Ireland and Scotland and have done as much as could be exepcted by me in the time.

"Altho' ye amount is nothing adequate to my labor, yet I have the satisfaction to think I have contributed my share of fatigue for ye advancement of Religion and learning in America. My anxiety to see you increases every day as ye time approaches, when, I shall not be separated again from you, but by ye last Debt of Nature.

"I set off tomorrow for London and only stay this Day here to write letters to different parts of Ireland and America. As I have many to write they ought to be very short.

"The Post Offices here are not so regular and punctual as one would expect. A letter from you with one from Mrs. Sergeant and another from Dr. Allison, all dated 17th July last, came to my hands but 2 days ago, altho' they arrived in London in August last. I have punctually given a particular account of all my motions as I had opportunity. Do not stop writing to me till you hear of my taking passage, because any letters that may come to me after my departure, can easily be sent after me.

"I have an offer of a passage both from Belfast and Derry gratis which would save 25 or 30 guineas to the Academy could I embrace it. Public measures seem to be at a stand here and ye ministry seem desirous of trying another year whether ye Americans will submit or not before they accommodate matters. It is said here that Lord North's Conciliatory Plan is sent over to ye Colonies for their opinion before it be enacted into a law. I know not what foundation there is for the report. The conduct of New York Assembly has given ye ministry great hopes of breaking ye union of the Colonies and thereby carrying their point at least. If America be now enslaved it will lie at their door.

"I hate these Politics that have ruined our mission and therefore will say no more about them. I am my dear,
"Yours affectionately,
"JOHN EWING."

Fifth Letter.

"LONDON, 9th July, 1775.

"MY DEAR:—

"I have nothing material to write you at this time save that I am setting my face homeward and now expect soon to be settled down in peace with you without ye prospect of being obliged to submit to another separation.

"I am surprised that I have had no letters from you by any of ye vessels that arrived here lately from Phil'a. Had not Mr. Bryan, my faithful correspondent wrote to me I should have heard nothing about you or the family, and also he tells me he will write no more to me from an apprehension that I shall have sailed before his letters reach me. I have not yet fixed the time of my sailing, but resolve that I will not put it off as to be late in the fall. I am waiting to see what effect his Majesty's donation will have to engage others to follow his example in contributions to our Academy, or whether I shall succeed in an application I am making for a Grant of Lands for ye Academy from ye King. When this is done, I resolve to sail without further delay, unless our prospects of success should grow very much better than they have been, so that in the judgment of our friends, I ought to stay a little longer. There is, however, very little hope of this, unless the Congress should make some proposals of an healing nature to ye King and his Ministers, they would be glad to accept of almost any terms rather than carry the dispute any farther and involve the country in civil war. They were greatly distressed with the blood that has already been shed in the two skirmishes that have already occurred and the disgrace their troops have met with in their encounter with men whom they have been taught to look upon as cowards who would not fight. Our success depends entirely on the accommodation of our Public Measures; should that take place speedily, we shall yet get as much money as will establish our Academy upon a permanent and solid foundation, and I am afraid this will not be the case, if I leave the business before it be completed.

"I am getting a few things for you and ye children to bring over with me. They must not be talked of on account of ye new Importation Agreement, lest I should find difficulty in bringing them ashore. I am thinking of some books for ye children and a piece of silk for gowns, etc.

"I have no directions for Mr. Sergeant as he knows my affairs now better than I do myself and I have the most perfect confidence in him to do everything that he knows would be for my advantage. Had I anything to say to him I would write. Yet I will if I have time write him a letter about politics and another to Mr. Bryan who will show you the state of this country. I am with kindest regards to all our friends,

"Yours affectionately,
"JOHN EWING."

The Billy whose education he was concerned about was his oldest son and named after John's oldest brother, William who had inherited the family estate in Maryland.

Hannah was the mother of eleven children and survived her husband 4 years dying at the home of her son, James Sergeant Ewing. The Assembly's magazine of April, 1806, has this item:—

"Departed this life, on Monday the 17th of March last at the residence of her son, Dr. James Sergeant Ewing, in Pittstown, New Jersey, in he 68th year of her age, Mrs. Hannah Ewing, relict of the Rev. John Ewing, D.D., late Senior Pastor of the first Presbyterian Church in Philadelphia and Provost of the University of Pennsylvania. This memorable lady, supported by that religion, of which she was an ornamental professor, endured a long and tedious illness with truly christian submission. Her remains were brought to this city and respectfully interred on the Thursday following, in the cemetery belonging to the First Presbyterian Congregation by the side of her husband. Mrs. Ewing was deservably esteemed by those who had the pleasure of her acquaintance; she was the affectionate wife, the anxious mother, and the sincere friend. Free now from the cares of this 'vale of tears' her spirit is made happy with her God.

"'Faith builds a bridge from this world to the next,
"'O'er death's dark gulph and all its horror hides.'"

Women are not called or considered "relicts" in this day but no doubt my great-grandmother would not have objected to being the relict of John Ewing, but perhaps had she lived in this day she would hardly have been venerable at seventy years, when many women are just beginning to live.

I have never thought of my great-grandfather as a poet, but recently the following poem was sent to me copied from an old *Port Folio* with a note. The following lines were found among the papers of Dr. Ewing in his own handwriting and we have not hesitated to ascribe them to his pen, because among other reasons, he was at one period of his life, very intimate with a gentleman, whose name is so affectionately commemorated in these stanzas:

(The poem follows):—

Why did the sun refuse to shine
On that black day that fix'd the line
And left me here to mourn
The absence of my dear De Witt
In lonely Anguish thus to sit
Till blessed with his return?

Say, Cupid, why he drew that face
In artless ease and softest grace,
With so much skill and art?
Contented with the bare profile,
Why did th' unfeeling painter smile
And overlook the heart?

Sure, when he saw this bosom rise,
And gaz'd so often on these eyes,
And every feature drew,
He could not fail to read this heart,
Untaught to act a double part,
But opened to his view.

Ah, shall I ne'er forget the hour
My eyes confess'd your sov'reign pow'r,
  My blushing cheeks grew warm;
Unusual transports thrill my frame,
My flitting colour, went and came—
  I dreaded future harm.

I saw yon guide, his trembling hand
And give new life, when at a stand,
  To finish the design;
He looked, he gaz'd, he paused, he drew,
As he was moved and taught by you
  To soften every line.

How could his flatt'ring pencil trace
Such unknown beauties in my face,
  Without thy heav'nly art?
Yet what has all thy skill availed?
These borrowed charms, alas! have failed
  To reach his callous heart!

Say, Cupid, hast thou lost thy art,
And did thy polished burning dart,
  That seldom fails to hit,
In spite of all thy well known skill,
Fly disobedient to thy will,
  When levelled at De Witt?

Or was the cruel sport designed
To pang my unsuspecting mind
  In that ill-fated hour?
Ah, Cupid, seek some other game—
Go, learn the savage heart to tame,
  That yet defies thy power.

Cupid replied, my art's entire;
I set thy bosom all on fire
  To place thy charms in view,
De Witt observed at my command,
He sketched thee with unerring hand,
  And felt my dart was true.

The fine portrait of Dr. Ewing in the University of Pennsylvania was painted by De Witt, the artist to whom this poem was written.

It gives us another side to this scientist-educator-clergyman and astronomer. He must have written other poems in his leisure hours but how could he ever have had *leisure* hours?

It is an old saying that those who do the most have time for everything. We are reminded also of the Indian Chief who called on the Senator who told him he had no time to attend to him and the Indian replied, "Why you have all the time there is."

CHAPTER III.

DR. EWING AS AN ASTRONOMER.

For the Port Folio, 1824.

LETTER from the Rev. Mr. Maskelyne, Astronomer Royal of England to the Rev. Dr. John Ewing, late Provost of the University of Pennsylvania.

Mr. Oldschool, A correspondent in one of our daily Gazettes, speaking of the two Comets, which at present excite so much attention, concludes with the following remarks: "In looking over the first volume of our Philosophical Transactions, I feel a sentiment of pride and pleasure that the occurrence of the transit of Venus in 1769 was observed with so much accuracy and precision in Pennsylvania, as to deserve and obtain the highest praise from the European astronomers.

"It is true, we cannot now, as we could then boast of a Rittenhouse whose genius was pre-eminent, but he had several coadjutors who without *pretending* to his *abilities,* were yet correct and scientific; and I hope it will not be found that we have in any respect degenerated."

I know not the grounds upon which this writer has ventured to place Mr. Rittenhouse above others who observed the transit of Venus at the time here specified. Certainly there is nothing like it in the work which he cites. On the contrary, Mr. Rittenhouse appears in that volume as the coadjutor of Dr. William Smith, in conjunction with whom he made observations at Norristown in the neighborhood of this City. He reported his results to

Dr. Smith and this gentleman made the communication to the Philosophical Society, from which institution it is presumed, they derived their appointment.

It appears from the 1st Vol. of the "Transactions" that the whole design originated with Dr. Ewing; and there is reason to believe that the prosecution of it, through all the details to the final result, was confided to him. His communication to the Society, dated 21st June, 1768, commences in these words—"As you have taken under consideration the proposal which I made to you the 19th of April last, of observing the ensuing transit of Venus," etc.

Dr. Ewing then proceeds to lay before the Society a projection of the transit as seen from Philadelphia, together with the elements of the projection and he concluded by proposing that provision be made, without loss of time, for erecting a small observatory, and he recommends that some proper persons be appointed to make the observations, at the expense of the Society, etc. The tone, of the letter throughout is that of one who is better acquainted with the subject than those whom he addresses; and who is obliged to take some pains to convince them of the importance of his suggestions. A conjecture which will not be considered very unwarrantable when the reader is informed that the same volume contains a method of destroying wild garlic, another of preserving peas from the worms—a third for preserving subjects in spirits; together with instructions for putting up seeds and plants for transportation, and various other valuable matters. Not many years after this event in 1773, Dr. Ewing and his friend Dr. Williamson, went to England to solicit pecuniary aid in behalf of the Newark Academy in Delaware. Although the war of the revolution was just breaking out, they were treated with the utmost cordiality and many liberal subscriptions were received.

The reputation of Dr. Ewing had prepared for him a cordial reception in the closets of the literary and learned of that day, with many of whom he maintained a correspondence several years after his return. By Lord North, the minister, the most liberal offers were made to induce him to remain in that country. While he was in London he made some efforts to procure the means of establishing an observatory in this City.

The Rev. Mr. Maskelyne then Astronomer-Royal at Greenwich was applied to, and the reply of that eminent person will show the estimation in which our young American philosopher was held, by an individual who of all the men then living, was best qualified to decide upon the pretensions of others in this department of science.

It is in the following words:

"GREENWICH, 4th Aug., 1775.

"SIR:—I received your late favour, together with your observations of the comet of 1770 and some copies of that of 1769, for which I thank you. I shall, I believe, communicate them to the Royal Society as you give me leave. In the present unhappy situation of American affairs, I have not the least idea that anything can be done towards erecting an observatory at Philadelphia and therefore cannot think it proper for me to take a part in any memorial you may think proper to lay before my Lord North at present. I do not mean however, to discourage you from presenting a memorial from yourself.

"Were an observatory to be erected at that City, I do not know any person there more capable of taking care of it than yourself. Should Lord North do me the honour to ask my opinion about the utility of erecting an observatory at Philadelphia, I should then be enabled to speak out, being always a well wisher to the promotion of science.

You did not distinguish whether the times of your observations were apparent or mean time.

"I am Sir

"Your most humble Servant,

"N. Maskelyne.

"To the Rev. Dr. Ewing, at No. 25 Ludgate Street."

The observations were engraved on a sheet of large paper, of which it is supposed a number of copies were sent to Mr. M.

O. O.

The City Councils, at the earnest solicitation of the American Philosophical Society granted the rise of the edifice in Center Square for this purpose several years ago. But nothing has been done with the premises, that we know of by the Society.

O. O.

"At the period when this letter was written, a reputation for science was to be acquired only by real merit. A membership in a learned institution was not then voted in return for a donation of books or sheets, nor had it become an article of trade, as it is now, when an exchange of titles between two persons, members of different societies can be calculated on, with nearly the same confidence as a return of tea for a cargo of dollars.

"Dr. Ewing as well as Dr. Rittenhouse, was a modest man, whose labours were prompted by a love, science and zeal for the public good. Whether his observations were communicated to the Royal Society, as Mr. Maskelyne proposed, I never heard. Had he been sedulous of notoriety, there is no doubt that he could have obtained the envied privilege of adding F. R. S. to his name. It is known that his high character for learning procured for him a vote of the freedom of several cities in Scotland where learning was held in high estimation. That custom has gone out of use abroad, and in our own country, we seem little disposed to honour any art or science but that which teaches us the most direct road to wealth or political power. Men of solid worth are driven into the shade and their places are filled by charlatans, who play the zany in newspapers and shake their caps and bells at fish-feasts.

"Before I conclude, it may not be amiss to add that it is by no means my object to disparage the merits of our self-taught philosopher. They were of a high order and none knew them better or valued them more justly, than the individual whose claims I have undertaken to vindicate."

This was probably written by the Editor of the Port Folio John E. Hall, who was Dr. Ewing's grandson.

The children of John and Hannah Sergeant Ewing:

1. MARY, b. 1759;
2. SARAH, b. 1761; d. 1830; m. John Hall.
3. WILLIAM, b. 1763; d. 1810; m. Elizabeth Wallace, 1st wife; Mrs. Braxton, second.
4. ANN, b. 1766; m. William Davidson.
5. JAMES SERGEANT EWING, b. 1770; m. Catherine Otto.
6. ELIZABETH, b. 1772; m. Robert Harris.
7. SAMUEL, b. 1776; d. 1825; m. Elizabeth Redman;
  His twin brother
8. JOHN, m. Magdalene Johnson.
9. MARGARET, b. 1777.
10. AMELIA, b. 1782.
11. HANNAH, b. 1786.

William Ewing was Dr. John Ewing's eldest son. He is the Billy spoken of in the letters his father writes from Great Britain to his wife in Philadelphia. "As we shall be able to give them little or no fortune, they should have as good learning as we can give them. I hope Billy keeps close to his ciphering and that he takes so much delight in it as to make progress."

Billy became a lawyer and was married first to Elizabeth Wallace, His second wife was Mrs. Braxton, the widow of Fitzhugh Braxton, 4th son of the signer of the Declaration of Independence, Carter Braxton, and grandson of King Carter of Virginia as he was called.

There was a son William by his second marriage, and one of his granddaughters lives in this city and another is married and lives in Brooklyn.

Elizabeth Ewing married Robert Harris the son of John Harris the founder of Harrisburg, and her father thought so much of his son-in-law he left him his gold headed cane which had been given to him by his friend Dr. Johnson when he was in Great Britain for two years getting money for the Newark Academy.

It was stipulated the cane should descend in the male line but the Harrises had no son, so it has come down to Elizabeth's granddaughter Mrs. Louisa Wilson of Philadelphia.

Dr. James Sergeant Ewing was the fifth child of Dr. John Ewing.

He married Catherine a daughter of Bode Otto, one of the most distinguished physicians of his time, and an officer in the Revolutionary Army. Her brother Dr. John C. Otto was also an eminent physician and medical professor of Philadelphia for nearly fifty years.

There were three children of this union:

JACOB OTTO EWING and two daughters, AMELIA and CATHERINE.

Dr. J. S. Ewing lived near Fifth and Chestnut Sts., and

in later years on Broad St., near Spruce, spending the summers near Trenton.

When his daughter Amelia was advanced in years, the sole survivor of her family, it was my privilege to make her many visits. She had a country house on the outskirts of Newtown, a beautiful garden and farm attached. She was the lady of the Manor with her servants and her cats, and a charming companion. She was an unusually fine character loving flowers and books, and administering to many charities in the most unostentatious manner. Her home was the last word in comfort, but she rarely spent money on herself. It was always of others she was thinking, how she might best aid them. The people about her thought her very extravagant and when her cook became somewhat delicate in health and she engaged another and allowed the old one to remain, their astonishment knew no bounds and I feel sure a few were quite horrified. I was usually invited up the last week in April and I shall never forget our early trips to the garden to see the hyacinths and tulips peeping up in the cold and defying the spring winds. Cousin Amelia took such an interest in each one, and many times a day we visited the garden to watch the glory of the miracle of that last week in April, the loveliest of all the year, blossom time, and the delicate green of the early spring.

In doors were many beautiful things, her father had brought from India and China and other places he visited and I am fortunate enough to have become the possessor of some of them, to remind me of the dear lady.

One day when she was eighty years old or as Oliver Wendell Holmes would say "eighty years young," I saw her very intent upon a book and asked her what she was reading, she replied "I am studying my Italian lesson for the day." Not many ladies of eighty study the languages in our time, and that was only one of the many subjects she was interested in. She was so concerned about the women of India that at last she consented to part with her beloved companion who was like a daughter. But she never considered how she would miss her and the long letters that came to her from India were her compensation when she learned of the work being done for the women of that wonderfully civilized and also uncivilized country. Miss Amelia Ewing was a remarkable character and a worthy granddaughter of Dr. John Ewing.

It was at her father's home where her grandmother, Mrs. Hannah Sergeant Ewing spent her last days as she survived her husband several years.

John Ewing, the twin brother of Samuel, was also a lawyer. He married Magdalene Johnson, whose family lived opposite the Chew House in Germantown and from the garden was fired that first gun into the celebrated mansion. Magdalene's sister was the mother of Mrs. Samuel Chew.

John and Magdalene left two daughters, Elizabeth and Ellen Ewing who made their home for some years with their uncle Washington Harris in Harrisburg.

When they came back to Philadelphia they opened a school for girls and later on grew weary of teaching and kept an old fashioned boarding house at 1104 Spruce St. They were estimable women and after inheriting money which enabled them to retire and live quietly, spent much of their time reading to the sick in the hospitals of Philadelphia.

CHAPTER IV.
SARAH EWING (Mrs. John Hall).

SARAH and her brother Samuel were the two children of John Ewing and Hannah Sergeant who most resembled their father intellectually. We cannot say inherit, as scientists tell us today we do not inherit directly from our parents, but from a common ancestor. This daughter was the fifth child, born October 30th, 1761. She was fifteen years older than her gifted brother Samuel, so that her son, John E. Hall, was very near the age of his uncle.

In an era when women usually exercised their minds in domestic and social matters with occasional reading, Sarah Ewing Hall became the greatest woman writer of her day in America.

We can imagine the atmosphere of her early home life: The broad culture and religious training and the contact with the learned and brilliant people who constantly visited her father, distinguished in so many lines. She studied astronomy with him, who loved to impart his knowledge, making frequent observations with him and continued through life to improve the knowledge she had first gained from him. She also acquired an extensive acquaintance with the classics by listening to her brothers recite their Latin and Greek lessons to their father. When she was twenty-one, she married John Hall, the son of a wealthy planter in Maryland, who had come over with Lord Baltimore. They lived for eight years upon a beautiful estate on the shores of the Susquehanna.

But Mrs. Hall was not accustomed to a country life, and

SARAH EWING
Mrs. John Hall

even the beauty of the Susquehanna could not compensate for the companionship of her father and the coterie of literary and scientific people who surrounded him. She had a wonderful inquiring mind. Constantly seeking knowledge of the great things in life and enjoying the discussions on all subjects. She loved books, society and her friends. So they came back to Philadelphia. Mr. Hall was Secretary to the Land Office and United States Marshal for the District of Pennsylvania.

From this time on she led a very active life with the cares of homekeeping and many children, duties which it is said were never neglected. She thoroughly enjoyed her many social activities so that in order to carry on her beloved reading and study she waited until all the family had retired and for the last forty years of her life was accustomed to engage her mind in mental work until two and often three o'clock A. M. She must have possessed the same strong and healthy mind and constitution as her father and it was said of him he had never had an ill day in sixty years.

When Dennie established the Port Folio in 1800, Mrs. Hall was one of the literary circle with whom he associated and to whose pen that magazine was indebted for its celebrity. To contribute to the Port Folio was considered no small honor, for among the writers were a number of gentlemen who afterwards filled the most exalted stations in the Federal Government, in the Cabinet, on the Bench, and in various ways have reaped the highest rewards of patriotism and genius. It is said some of the most sprightly essays and pointed criticisms which were published in this magazine at the time of its greatest popularity were from the pen of Mrs. Hall. She possessed both wit and humor and her contributions could readily be distinguished by their vivacity as by the classic purity of their diction. In 1806 her gifted and oldest son, John Elihu Hall, became Editor of the Port Folio and for ten years his mother aided him until the magazine was discontinued in 1827, shortly before their death.

The following lines are written in "Lives of Eminent Philadelphians":—

John Elihu Hall.

John E. Hall was born December, 1783. He was educated at Princeton, read law with Judge Hopkinson, was admitted to practice in 1805 and removed to Baltimore. He published "The American Law Journal" in Philadelphia from 1808 to 1817. He was elected Professor of Rhetoric and Belles-Letters in the University of Maryland.

He collected and arranged an edition of "The British Spy," to which he contributed several letters, much to the gratification of Wirt, the author. When the Baltimore riot broke out in 1811, he was one of the party of Federalists who aided in defending Hanson's house, and was one of the nine thrown on a heap as killed. He left Baltimore soon afterwards, removing to Philadelphia, where he assumed the Editorship of the Port Folio in 1806. "The Memoires of Anacreon" in that journal, were from his pen. They were a reproduction on his thread of narrative, of Grecian manners and customs, supposed to be written by critics of Athens and the author was stimulated to their composition by the approval of the poet Moore, who was then creating a sensation in the literary circles of Philadelphia. Mr. Hall was the author of the Life prefixed to the poems of his friend Dr. John Shaw, published in Baltimore in 1810.

In 1827, he edited with biographical and critical notes,

"The Philadelphia Souvenir," a collection of fugitive pieces from the press of that city.

The Editor's part is written with spirit. In the same year was published in Philadelphia in an octavo volume, "Memoirs of Eminent Persons, with Portraits and Facsimiles, written and in part selected by the Editor of the Portfolio."

In consequence of his declining health, the Portfolio was discontinued in 1827. He died June 11th, 1829, in the forty-sixth year of his age.

From "Lives of Eminent Philadelphians":—

In Mr. Hall's book "The Philadelphia Souvenir" he has written a sketch of his uncle, Samuel Ewing, and inserted his poems, among them the one written on the departure of his friend, Tom Moore, from America.

Mr. Hall was a great admirer of his uncle, who was only his elder by seven years.

Mrs. Hall began the Conversations on the Bible after she had passed fifty, taking up the study of Hebrew to make the necessary and accurate researches for the work. The success of the book was far beyond her modest expectation. It passed into four large editions, the third of which was published in London with eminent success.

Her son, Harrison Hall of Philadelphia, wrote of her that "She studied with all the humility of christian zeal and with the scholar's thirst for acquisition and became as eminent for scholarship in this department of learning as she was for wit, vivacity and genius. Few men, even among professional theologians, excelled her in knowledge of the Holy Scriptures."

The Conversations were widely read and are to be found today in the Ridgway Library. Mr. Harrison Hall published a little book of her essays in 1833, three years after her death. Some of them were written for the Port Folio. In "Reminiscencies of Philadelphia," she describes the Assembly:—

"This was held once a fortnight, and managed by six married gentlemen of the most respectable rank and character. This association, it must be confessed, partook of the aristocratic feeling infused into our community by a monarchical government. The families of mechanics, however wealthy, were not admitted. The subscription was £3-15s and admitted the master and the females of his family. Young men never appeared there under the age of twenty-one, and then they paid for their own tickets. Young ladies could not be introduced under eighteen.

"Supper at the Assembly consisted of tea, chocolate and rusk, a simple cake, now never seen amidst the profusion of confectionery that inundates our entertainments. We had at that time no spice of French in our institutions; consequently we did not know how to romp in cotillions, but moved with grave dignity in minuets, and sober gaiety in country dances. Everything was conducted by rule and order; places were distributed by lot, and partners were engaged for the evening, and neither could be changed by either forwardness or favoritism. Gentlemen always drank tea with their partners the day after the Assembly.

"Private balls were sometimes given; tea parties were not known by that term, yet by the established modes of visiting, ten or a dozen ladies were often collected, to partake of that pleasant beverage."

This book reflects the manners and customs and thought of the times and showing the keen and lively interest Mrs. Hall had on every subject. Even fashions, and as this little chapter, I am sure, will interest some of my readers very much, I am moved to quote it entire. It shows her versatility more than anything else, that the lady who woke up and found herself famous for her "Conversations on the Bible," should condescend to champion women's fashions, is quite delightful. This was written for the Port Folio:—

"On Fashion.

"Addressed to the Editor of the Portfolio.

"Most of you writers have leaped into the censor's throne without leave or license; where you were no sooner seated than, with the impudence one might expect from such conduct, you have railed with all the severity of satire and indecency of invective against our folly, frivolity, forwardness, fondness of dress and so forth. You can't conceive what a latitude is assumed by the witlings of the day, from the encouragement of such pens as your's. Those well dressed young gentlemen who will *lay awake whole nights* in *carving* the *fashions* of a new doublet, and who will criticise Cooper without knowing whether Shakespeare wrote dramas or epic poems: these wiseacres, I say, saunter along Chestnut Street when the sun shines, and amuse themselves with sneers against our sex, and in nothing are we so much the object of their ridicule as in our devotion to fashion, on whose shrine, according to these modern peripatetics, we sacrifice our time, our understanding, and our health. We have freedom of the press and freedom of religion, and why should we not enjoy a freedom of fashions?

"What do these sapient gentlemen wish? Would they have a dress for females established by an act of the Assembly, as doctors of medicine have been created in Maryland? 'Which dress aforesaid of the aforegoing figure, color, materials, fashion, cut, make, etc., etc., all the good spinsters of Pennsylvania shall wear on all highdays, and holidays under pain etc., etc.' Horrible idea! What! tie us down to the dull routine of the same looks, the same bonnets, the same cloak? take from us that charming diversity, that delightful variety, which blooms in endless succession from week to week, with the changes of the season; make us tedious to ourselves, and as unalterable, and unattractive as an old family picture—or what is equally out of the way and insipid, an old Bachelor? Rob us of half our charms and deprive us of all the subjects of thought and conversation. You men may talk of your dogs, your horses and your wine; but alas! if you take fashion from us, pray Mr. Saunter inform me upon what topic shall we converse with our beaux? Can you furnish any substitute for the delightful themes of ribands, laces, bonnets, shawls, new dresses with all the delightful inquiries, about the forms and fashions intended to be at Mrs. O.'s party tomorrow night or which agitated the bosoms of so many belles on the preceding evening at Mrs. T.'s? We should really mope ourselves into the melancholy of a young lawyer who looks and sighs in vain for a mistress or a client, or a gay girl who is shut up in the country enjoying the poetical charms of turbid ponds, bellowing cattle and neighbourly, visitations; and the poor dear little Dandies for lack of new bonnets and gay ribands to talk about, would relapse into downright torpitude.

"But some of you talk of simplicity of nature; of the gew gaw display of artificial charms, or deforming nature's works by the cumberous and fantasticle enbellishments of art and so forth.

"Now, sir, if you will pin the argument to this point, I shall have you in my power. Pray is nature simple, barren tedious, dull, uniform and unadorned as you old bachelors would have us to be, so that we might resemble your comfortless selves? Look at the trees, are they all of the same color? Are they not so infinitely diversified in their shades and figures, that to an observing eye, no two are alike? Observe the flowers of the garden: do they exhibit the same sombre or pale hue?

"Do they present that dull simplicity which you recommend to us, whom your gravest philosophers allow to be the handsomest beings in creation?

"Do you prefer the dull uniformity of a trench of upright celery to the varigated bed of tulips? What would you say of a project to reform nature by robbing the rose of its blushing red, the lily of its silver lustre, the tulip of its gorgeous streaks, the violet of its regal purple and allowing the vale to be no longer embroidered with their various beauties? or, of blotting from the clouds their golden streaks and dazzling silver, and banishing the gay rainbow from the heavens because they are not of a uniform color, but forever present more varieties and combinations of beauties than our imagination can paint? And shall not we, who, at least, pretended to have the gift of reason imitate nature? Nature has given for our use the varied dyes of the mineral and vegetable world, which enables us almost to vie with her own splendid gilding. Nature made us to be various, changeable, inconstant, many colored, whimsical, fickle and fond of show, if you please, that we follow nature with the greatest fidelity, when, like her, we use her beauties to delight the eye, gratify the taste and employ the mind in the harmonious varieties of color and figure to which fashion resorts, and to which we devote so much time and thought.

"Attend to these hints, and if you properly digest them, I have no doubt so sensible a head as you possess must nod assent to my doctrine that to study fashion and be in the fashion is the most delightful and harmless employment upon earth and the most conformable to our nature. But, if you should be so perverse as to think erroneously on this subject, I advise you to keep your observations to yourself, or to have your head well wigged the next time you come amongst us."

Finding a copy of the "Conversations on the Bible" in the Philadelphia Library, I thought I would look it over, not expecting to read it, but I read it through to the end. It is a most fascinating story of the Old Testament written in Mrs. Hall's delightful manner and you are impressed with the scholarship and knowledge she had of her subject. I am not surprised it made her famous here and in London.

Young people are not brought up to read the Bible now, but if this book could be given to them as part of their education, it would certainly give them an interest in the Book of Books they would not be likely to get in any other way.

John Ewing must always have been proud of his distinguished daughter, but it would have made him more so had he lived longer and known of this her greatest achievement.

Her sons also were worthy of their distinguished grandfather and brilliant mother. Besides John Elihu, the Editor of the Port Folio, Harrison (1785-1866), published the Portfolio for a time and wrote a work on Distillation commended by eminent scientists; James (1793-1868) after a notable career in the War of 1812 and in the Algerian Expedition went West, became a newspaper editor, Judge and Treasurer of Illinois and historian of the Middle West. Thomas Mifflin Hall was a surgeon and contributed poetry and scientific articles to the Portfolio 1798-1828.

SAMUEL EWING

The original sketch by Albert Rosenthal from an old portrait

CHAPTER V.

SAMUEL EWING.

SAMUEL EWING was born in 1776 when his father was 44. When the "Ewings" are cited in Literary Annals he is the one who is included with his father. He was the 7th child and the elder of his twin brother John. It is curious that both he and his father had a twin brother.

He inherited the same love of books and educational pursuits but while religion, science, philosophy and mathematics attracted the father's mind, Samuel inclined to Poetry, Literature, Music, Drama and Art.

To be sure he chose the law as his profession in which he became eminent in his day. But like his father he was able to do many things and do them well, as his friend, Thomas I. Wharton, in "Lives of Eminent Philadelphians," so very beautifully pictures him. We must quote the sketch as the writer feels she must give place to the one who knew him and was able to describe him far better than she, as he died when his son, her father, was only seven years old. The writer was always impressed, however, with the adoration her father had for her grandfather, and one of his delightful memories was being carried to Belmont in his father's arms to visit Judge Peters in his beautiful home on the hill overlooking the river and the city in its narrow confines as it was in that day.

Samuel was a great book collector and many of his treasures are in the writer's possession with the name, S. Ewing, in each book or Set of first American Editions.

His Shakespeare in 17 Vols. published in 1805 is one of the chief treasures of the Collection.

Written by Thomas I. Wharton and published in "Lives of Eminent Philadelphians":—

"Samuel Ewing who became the third Vice-President of the Athenaeum of Philadelphia, was the son of Dr. Ewing, sometime Provost of the University, at which institution he received a liberal education, which he improved by very extensive reading. He became a member of the legal profession, and attained considerable success and distinction, without ceasing to bestow a portion of his time in the cultivation of the garden of letters. Mr. Ewing was a contemporary, and a literary associate and friend of Dennie, the Editor of the Portfolio, to whose memory he was warmly attached: and one of that Company of men of wit and accomplishments, whom Moore, the poet describes in his beautiful verses as 'the sacred few, whom late by Delaware's green banks I knew.'

"He became, afterwards, the Editor of a magazine, composed, principally of republications from English reviews and other periodicals. Mr. Ewing was remarkable, during his whole life, for the kindness of his friendship, his social disposition, and conversational powers. He would have been a welcome member of those literary clubs in which wits and writers of London have delighted to congregate.

"Mr. Ewing died in the month of February, 1825, after a lingering illness, having lived just long enough to hear of and rejoice in the election of his old friend and literary companion, Mr. John Quincy Adams, to the office of President of the United States."

In the same book we have a sketch of the life of the writer of the above, and we insert it as it shows that this appreciation of Mr. Ewing was written by one who was very eminent himself in the same qualities he accords to his friend.

"Thomas I. Wharton, was born in Philadelphia, in April, 1791, and died in the same city in March, 1856. He was at the time of his death a leading member of the Philadelphia Bar, having made real estate his specialty, and having acquired an experience in that branch of jurisprudence which enabled his naturally keen and discriminatory mind, to act with equal promptness and accuracy on the delicate and difficult questions of title, of which towards the end of his life he was almost the sole professional arbiter.

"Few of his cotemporaries equalled him in general scholarship; still fewer, in that literary taste and skill, which placed him, as a writer, in a position which it is only to be regretted that his great fastidiousness of temper, and his heavy pressure of other labor, prevented him from improving. Of severe integrity, and of almost excessive delicacy, in questions of social and political propriety, his walk was limited to his family and business relations, beyond which with but few exceptions, his associations were only formal. These exceptions were the main literary foundations of Philadelphia, in several of which, viz., the Philosophical and Historical Societies, the Library and Athenaeum Companies, he was among the most active members."

There is a special charm about men of letters, judicious reading and thinking give them a variety of interests and produce usually a sympathetic understanding of people and things and they are apt to be delightful conversationalists. On the other hand the scientist and specialist may be more useful in one groove in which they have an absorbing interest and to which they sacrifice most of their time.

Every profession, pursuit and trade has its own special

use and as Browning says, "All service ranks the same with God." But the man of Letters lives a fuller and richer life and is just as useful as he sheds an enlightening culture that gives joy and pleasure to those with whom he comes in contact, especially to those who appreciate the finer things of life even though they have not had the time to follow up themselves."

Samuel Ewing was one of the founders of the Academy of Fine Arts and his name is enrolled in the old parchment, which of late years, we notice is found copied in the catalogues of the Annual Exhibits. He was also one of the founders of Musical Fund Hall, and one of the three connected with the opening of the New Theater in the early days of the Nineteenth Century. Mention has also been made of the Athenaeum of which he was the third Vice-President.

John E. Hall, who edited the Port Folio after Dennie, says in his Biographical Sketch, published in "The Philadelphia Souvenir" that "Samuel Ewing was one of those who, with talents which might achieve an elevated rank in National Concerns, preferred the pursuits of an honorable profession and he frequently exhibited proofs of that fine combination of genius and humour which characterized both his conversation and his writings. Among his juvenile efforts may be mentioned a dramatic performance, which was never acted, because it was a political satire and the allusions too personal and pungent for the stage. He became a student in the Office of Wm. Lewis and was one of the "Earliest and most valuable correspondent of the Port Folio and was an ardent admirer and cordial friend of Mr. Dennie. The Reflections in Solitude which appeared occasionally in the columns of the Port Folio were sought with flattering eagerness and no reader in whose heart the muse of Cooper has found a place will perruse the Meditations of Jacques without emotion. Under this assumed name he surveys landscape with the eye of the painter and displays great felicity in combining sentiment with description.

Many of the most humorous among the prose essays were also from his various and fertile pen. He found leisure, also, to impart zest and vivacity to some of the daily gazettes, by pasquinades the effect of which was not forgotten by those who came under his lash."

In 1804, when Thomas Moore visited Philadelphia, Mr. Hall writes he found the Club of wits in the full enjoyment of healthy high spirits and literary zeal.

His poems had preceded him and been transplanted into the Port Folio and loudly extolled. The Evening hours which this junta enjoyed at Number 2, after the day had been devoted to severer studies made a strong impression upon the mind of Thomas Moore and his gratitude was afterwards expressed in a passage which may be introduced in this place as a beautiful tribute of genius to the powers of friendship and hospitality.

"To the Honorable
"W. R. Spencer,
from Buffalo on Lake Erie.

"Oh you sacred few
Whom late by Delaware's green banks I knew.

Whom known and lov'd through many a social eve,
'Twas bliss to live with and 'twas pain to leave!
Not with more joy the lonely exile scanned
The writing trac'd upon the desert sand,
When his lone heart but little hoped to find
One trace of life, one stamp of human kind.
Then did I trail the pure, the enlightn'd zeal,
The strength to reason and the warmth to feel
The manly polish and the illumin'd taste
Which mid the melancholy heartless waste

My foot has travers'd, Oh you sacred few,
I found by Delaware's green banks with you.
* * * * * * * * * *
It is to you, to souls that favouring Heaven
Has made like yours, the glorious task is given.
Oh, but for such, Columbia's days were done,
Rank without ripeness, quicken'd without sun,
Crude at the surface, rotten at the core,
Her fruits would fall, before her spring were o'er.

Believe me, Spencer, while I wrong the hours,
Where Schuylkill undulates thro' banks of flowers,
Though few the days, the happy evenings few,
So warm with heart, so rich with mind they flew,
That my full soul forgot its wish to roam,
And rested there as in a dream of home!
And looks I met like looks I met before,
And voices, too, which as they trembl'd o'er
The chord of memory, found full many a tone
Of kindness there in concord with thine own.
Yes, we had nights of that communion free,
That flow of heart which I have known with thee
So oft, so warmly; nights of mirth and mind,
Of whims that taught and follies that refin'd.
When shall we both renew them? When restor'd
To the gay feast and intellectual board,
Shall I once more enjoy with thee and thine
Those whims that teach, those follies that refine?
Even now as wandering upon Erie's shore
I hear Niagara's distant cataract roar;
I sigh for home—alas, these weary feet
Have many a mile to journey ere we meet."

After his return to England, Moore writes, "I wish you would tell Mr. Dennie and Mr. Ewing that nothing could give me greater happiness than to hear from them * * *" And again he writes, "It gives me great pleasure to find that you remember me so kindly and I would very willingly make my peace with those of your Countrymen who think otherwise of me. This life however is just long enough to commit errors in, but too short to allow no time to repair them and there are few of my errors I regard more sincerely, than the rashness I was guilty of, in publishing those crude and boyish tirades against the Americans.

And then follows the poem written by Samuel Ewing:—

POEM BY SAMUEL EWING.

Written after the departure of Thomas Moore from Phila.

How oft have I seen, at the first blush of morning,
    The wretch, to whose eyelids repose were a treasure,
Turn sad, on his pillow, and snatch a short slumber
    As fancy, the while, wove o'er visions of pleasure.

And then in his light-dreams all fleeting as showers
    That kiss the new grass in the morning of spring,
His fair one would smile as he sighed all his passion
    And blushing receive from his fingers the ring.

At a moment like this, the bright vision would vanish!
    In vain would he woo the soft god back again,
The dream of his fancy had gone, and he sigh'd
    That pleasure should fly from the footsteps of pain.

Thus, to me, youthful stranger! (whom fate has permitted
    To charm us, from friends and from country to roam)
Thyself wert the vision, that flitted before me,
    That stole to my bosom and made it a home.

But the rainbow of evening can linger not long,
    Its mellow tints fade, and we watch it in vain
And the rose bud that blooms in the morning of May
    Soon loses its sweets, but its thorns still remain.

And yet, if kind memory be doomed to revive
    In me the impressions, affection has wore,
I shall woo her to visit me oft, for I know
    She will show, in my day dreams, the image of Moore.

                                                                JACQUES.

Mr. Hall says that although Mr. Ewing sought the light of jurisprudence with all the assiduity of one whose spirit aspires to the rock of independence, a taste for literature distinguished him through life, and there is little doubt that if he had cultivated letters as an author, he would have attained eminence. In the year 1809, he projected a monthly miscellany, entitled "Select Reviews and Spirit of the Foreign Magazines." This work was published under his direction about three years, during which time it amply rewarded his attention and later on he disposed of his interest for a considerable sum.

Professional business which will admit of no rival at length began to reward his studies and his devotion to it was almost exclusive, for he was surpassed by no one in zeal for his clients. Hence his success at the bar.

He still continued to display his regard for learning by the active part he took in the establishment of the Athenaeum of Philadelphia and by the support and attention he afterwards bestowed upon that useful institution. He was early elected and annually re-elected unanimously a director and by the Board, the Vice-President of this Society. The utility of his labours and the estimation in which he was regarded by his associates are emphatically commemorated in the minute entered upon their records on the occasion of his demise; and his loss was again adverted to in impressive terms at the conclusion of the address which is made annually to the stockholders. The minute is in these words:

"Resolved: that the directors of the Athenaeum are deeply sensible of the loss, which they in common with the rest of their fellow citizens have sustained by the lamented death of their late Vice-President, Mr. Ewing, whose zealous exertions materially aided the foundation of the institution and to whose intelligence and activity its present prosperous condition is greatly owing."

Samuel Ewing had the poet's heart and worshipped beauty in all its manifestations. His first love was for the beautiful Rebecca Gratz and they would have married but for the difference in their religions which neither felt they could conscientiously give up.

He was the "Christian Gentleman" that allusion is made to as the beloved of the noble, philanthropic and beautiful Jewess.

There were three portraits of her painted by Sully and they were exhibited in his wonderful collection at the Academy of Fine Arts in the Spring of 1922: One was especially beautiful.

The fiancée of Washington Irving was her intimate friend and the four attractive and intelligent young people spent much of their time together, and Irving had a chance to know and appreciate the lovely qualities of the beautiful Miss Gratz.

On a visit to Walter Scott, the novelist talked of Ivanhoe and his desire to find a suitable character for his heroine, Irving said, "I know the very person for her," and told him of Rebecca Gratz and Scott made her the heroine of his famous novel. In 1810, Samuel Ewing married Elizabeth Redman; she was the daughter of Dr. Joseph Redman and Rebecca Bird, whose first husband was Peter Turner, a sister of Mrs. James Wilson, who was Rachel Bird.

So connecting the Wilson and Ewing families, whose descendants may have equal pride in the two distinguished heads, Dr. John Ewing and James Wilson the great jurist, the chief maker of the Constitution of the United States, of which the first rough draft in his handwriting may be seen in the Wilson Collection at the Historical Society of Pennsylvania, and whose life is shortly to be published in six volumes written by that distinguished scholar and Constitutional Historian of Pennsylvania, Burton Alva Konkle, who has so greatly illuminated our Colonial History.

Elizabeth Redman was also very beautiful, with titian hair and an exquisite complexion as we know from her mineature, painted when she was sixteen, and now in the possession of the Drayton family, as their daughter Julia Ewing married John G. Drayton, the creator of the beautiful Magnolia Gardens on the Ashley River 12 miles from Charleston, South Carolina. Elizabeth was not only beautiful but very musical. In the Wilson letters in the Historical Society, allusion is often made to her entertaining them and their guests with her delightful music. The Wilson children were her first cousins and almost like sisters as they lived near each other and often spent their summers together.

The Christ church records show they were confirmed on the same day and Mary Wilson who was much older alludes to her "Sweet little cousins," Elizabeth and her sister Maria, who married Samuel Nicholas. The first mention of my Grandfather's Courtship is in one of these letters. When Mary Wilson and her brother Bird, removed to Norristown, their first visitors a few days after the removal were Elizabeth and Samuel Ewing. That was in 1807, and later on Mary writes her friend Sally Chauncey, of New Haven, of her first two visitors in their new home.

They were married in 1810, and three of their children were named after the Wilson cousins, the writer's father Charles Henry Ewing being named after Mary's beloved brother who died young and who was particularly fond of his Cousin Elizabeth Redman.

When Samuel proposed to the beautiful Elizabeth, he told her he could not give her his first love but he would try to make her a good husband.

It is recorded in the family that once a month she took her children to call on Miss Gratz and when my Aunt was married she took her children to see the beautiful old lady, and when my cousin was a child she asked her mother why and what relation was between our families and Rebecca Gratz and she promised to tell her the story when she was grown up.

When my grandfather died she was ten and her sister fourteen and they stood at the door when the dear, loyal woman passed in and remained an hour. When she came out she left three white roses on his breast and her mineature on his heart.

I have always felt since knowing this story from my Aunt, the eye witness, that my grandmother must have been possessed of one very noble trait but perhaps with the happiness of being married to the distinguished man that she loved, enabled her to show to the lovely Rebecca the friendliness which in so many cases would have resulted otherwise.

Mr. Hall writes in his biography of Samuel Ewing that, "in private life, the manners and conversation of Mr. Ewing were brightly attractive, combining social feeling and frankness of temper, with sallies of playful wit. He was moreover, truly charitable and generous.

These qualities secured him the love of numerous personal friends; and his integrity as a man and usefulness as a citizen acquired the confidence of the community."

CHAPTER VI.

THE BIRDS OF BIRDSBORO.

WILLIAM BIRD and his son Mark were the Iron kings of Berks County. In 1740 or 1741 William built a forge and founded Birdsboro. Then he built a furnace at French Creek and at Roxborough. He is said to have owned 3000 acres, a grist mill and saw mill, besides his forges. In 1760 with other inhabitants of the County of Berks he petitioned the Society for the Propagation of the Gospel to send over a Missionary to reside in Reading, the chief town of the County aforesaid, and to officials also at Morlattrys, a place fifteen miles distant, where a church has for many years been built by a Society of English and Swedes, who are desirous of having a Missionary of the Church of England. Dr. William Smith, writing the Society 26 Aug., 1760, referring to the Petition said the first gentleman who signs, Mr. Bird, is worth 1000 guineas per annum in Iron Works.

I suppose 1000 guineas in 1760 was a large sum. He lived in a fine country seat on the Schuylkill where some of his iron works were established.

Mark Bird, the eldest of the children of William Bird, carried on and enlarged what his father had built up from 1740 until his death in 1762, when his son was 23 years old. He owned various properties at Reading, iron works at Birdsboro and Hopewell Furnace on Sixpenny Creek erected in 1765.

He manufactured shot and shells for the Continental

Army and was very active in the Revolution, fitting out three hundred men at his own expense.

He owned large property interests in New Jersey and Maryland and possessed 8000 acres of land.

In 1775 and 1776 Colonel Bird officiated as one of the Judges in the County Courts.

In 1763 he married Mary Ross, the sister of the Signer George Ross. It was a double wedding, his sister Rebecca marrying Peter Turner at the same hour. The ceremony was performed by Bishop White at Christ Church. It is said that James Wilson had a very high opinion of his brother-in-law's ability.

In 1788 Colonel Bird removed to North Carolina, where he died. James Wilson, who had married his sister Rachel Bird, became owner of his property. Edward Biddle, who had married Elizabeth Ross, his wife's sister, administered his estate.

Rebecca Bird, Mrs. Peter Turner, the writer's great-grandmother, was born in 1742, three years after her brother Mark. The Turners had one daughter, Juliana, and when she was six years old her father died.

Mrs. Turner figured much in the social gaieties of the time, and Silas Deane, who was an envoy to Paris, writes to her brother-in-law James Wilson he will execute promptly Mrs. Turner's commissions. A number of very beautiful brocade gowns were divided among her grandchildren, and the writer is fortunate enough to possess a strip of the very gorgeous crimson satin brocade in which she danced with the unfortunate but attractive Major Andre at the Mischianza.

Six year after Mr. Turner's death she married Dr. Joseph Redman, son of Joseph Redman, Esq., the well-beloved brother of Dr. John Redman.

Their daughters, Elizabeth married Samuel Ewing and

Maria became the wife of Samuel Nicholas, whose grandson Dr. J. Nicholas Mitchell died a few weeks ago in this city.

Juliana married William Miller. The family of the writer always called her "Auntie Miller," and many interesting stories were told of her visits to the Washingtons after they left Philadelphia. She brought home many gifts and mementoes of these visits, and when she was an old lady she invited the public to come and see them and charged 25 cents admission and gave the money to charity.

Her great-niece, Dr. Mitchell's sister, was named for her and inherited the collection. I well remember seeing the collection at my cousin's house when a young girl. One of the things which I remember best was a large cream pitcher with Washington's portrait on it, which I believe was one of a set belonging to the Washingtons, a gift to my great-aunt Miller. She was, like her mother, fond of social gaieties, and many traditions are in the family of her charming personality. She was petite but with such a stateliness of manner she gave the impression of height.

She grew up with the Wilson children, and being near Mary Wilson's age, was much with her. We read in the Wilson letters of their trip to Long Branch and rooming together, and when Juliana's husband died after a few days' illness Mary is with her in her sorrow. She lived long after Mary, seeing much of Bird Wilson, who survived all his family, passing away in 1855, while Bird Wilson died four years after.

She is buried in the Turner lot with her father and mother, while Dr. Redman, her step-father, is with the Redmans close by in Christ Church Cemetery.

Some of her little teaspoons and her copy of Hannah Moore have come down to the writer and are greatly treasured, especially as the book is marked in many serious passages—showing what interested her most.

Ann Pamela Cunningham and Her Grandfather, William Bird, Jr.

We do not know the date of his birth, but he was entered at the College of Philadelphia in 1769 several years after his brother Mark. He is noted as being the grandfather of our cousin, Miss Pamela Cunningham, who saved Mt. Vernon for the nation's shrine and was made its First Regent.

In a letter written in 1777 by his brother-in-law, James Wilson, to Major General Arthur St. Clair, he says:—

"If you have not already engaged yourself, you will much oblige me by appointing Billy Bird your aid-de-camp. You will recollect that when he first entered into service I was solicitous that he should be formed under you. You know, however, of his activity, he is young, but he is far from being perfect in sense and judgment. If he is not yet exchanged, I hope he soon will be. I have been informed that he has either obtained or has a prospect of obtaining a lieutenancy in the Light Horse. But I would on every account prefer what I now recommend him to.

"I have good reason to believe and think it not improper to hint that the important command of Ticonderoga is destined for your next campaign and presage it a theater of glory."

The Prediction Was Verified.

William Bird married Catherine, daughter of William Dalton, in Alexandria, Virginia, and was one of the vestrymen of Old Christ Church in that city. His daughter married Robert Cunningham, who was also a vestryman at the time Washington attended the historic old church, and Parmela Cunningham was the daughter of this marriage. When she was six years old she spent a week at Mt. Vernon with her mother, and naturally grew up with love for the home of the Washingtons.

Years after her mother, passing in a vessel going down the Potomac, saw the old mansion going to rack and ruin, and about to be sold. She was distressed, and sent the news to her daughter.

I have been told that our Cousin Pamela had a motto when there was anything difficult to be accomplished: "I will do it." She wrote this back to her mother. She was an invalid, but was carried from State to State, stirring up the country—especially the women. Then she besieged Congress, and we can well imagine the difficulty she had with that body. She at last conquered and the beautiful old home of the Father of his Country was saved. She was made First Regent. With all her activity she had a horror of publicity and was extremely modest, and that is why the country knows less about her than it should, for her life was a lesson of accomplishment, hampered by illness and lacking the freedom accorded to women today. Her name would today be placed among the number of greatest women in America.

William Bird had removed in 1790 to Georgia, and his daughter, Mrs. Robert Cunningham, lived in South Carolina in a beautiful old estate called Rosemont, near Laurens. The house, still standing, was made of logs cut from the Rosemont forest and sawed and framed in England. The little town of Cross Hill four miles from Rosemont has the honor of being the first contributor to the fund for the purchase of Mt. Vernon from Mr. John Augustine Washington.

In March, 1860, six years after Miss Cunningham sent the appeal to the country for $200,000 required for the purchase of Mt. Vernon, she invited both Houses of Congress to accompany the Association on its first official visit to the home and tomb of Washington. The invitation was accepted and the Senate passed a resolution to assemble on hour earlier than usual and to adjourn in season for the excursion.

On March 7th, with the Marine Band from the N Yard, the distinguished party left the wharf on the Thomas Collyer. In his address Hon. James P. Cochran, of New York, said:—

"The tomb in its dilapidated state was a matter of grief to every philanthropist, every patriot. The woman of America has achieved her desires, has accomplished her aims and Mt. Vernon, with its sacred ashes, reposes under the custody of the women of America, the property of the American Union." The contrast between that day and this is startling; the very atmosphere has been restored.

Mr. Lucas, of the London Times, wrote after a visit to Mt. Vernon last year:—

"We have no place of national pilgrimage in England that is so perfect a model as Washington's home at Mount Vernon. It is perhaps through lack of a figure of the Washington type that we have nothing to compare with it. I am filled with admiration."

Peggy Shippen writes "with broad vision and devoted patriotism, she saved her country from the reproach that the ruin and neglect of Mount Vernon must have cast upon it. But, after all, the founder's ideal in honoring with filial piety the memory of the maker of this great nation, has been realized."

A plaque at Mt. Vernon testifies to her efforts, and she will always be remembered as its saviour, and no doubt more and more appreciated as America is slowly learning to give praise where praise is due. The few who have vision do not wait for the opinion of a majority, but think for themselves. There is a beautiful tribute to Miss Cunningham in Scribner's "Point of View" for July, 1922, and Thomas Nelson Page published a little book on Mt. Vernon in 1910 which I am told is "out of print."

CHAPTER VII.

THE REDMANS.

1. Joseph Redman had two sons.
2. Joseph Redman, Esq., born 1719 and Dr. John Redman, 1722.
3. Dr. Joseph Redman, son of Joseph Redman, Esq.; m. Rebecca Turner, née Bird; two daughters, Elizabeth and Maria.

———o———

THE first record we have of the Redmans in America is a Joseph who is said to have been one of the first settlers in the State. He was the father of the great Dr. John Redman and his brother Joseph who was the writer's great-great-grandfather. There has been much written of Dr. John Redman. The following little sketch is in "Lives of Eminent Philadelphians."

"John Redman, M.D., first President of the College of Physicians of Philadelphia, was born in that city, February 27th, 1722. After finishing his preparatory education in Mr. Tennent's Academy, he entered upon the study of physic with John Kearsley, then one of the most respectable physicians of Philadelphia.

"When he commenced the practice of his profession, he went to Bermuda where he continued for several years, thence he proceeded to Europe for the purpose of perfecting his acquaintance with medicine. He lived one year in Edinburgh; he attended lectures, dissections and the hospitals in Paris; he graduated at Leyden in July, 1748, and after passing some time at Grey's Hospital, he returned to America and settled in his native city where he soon gained great and deserved celebrity. In the evening of his life he withdrew from the labors of his profession, but it was only to engage in business of another kind.

"In the year 1784 he was elected an elder of the Second Presbyterian Church, and the benevolent duties of this office employed him and gave him great delight. The death of his younger daughter in 1806 was soon succeeded by the death of his wife with whom he had lived near sixty years. He died of apoplexy March 19th, 1808, aged eighty-six years."

His portrait hangs in the great gallery of the College of Physicians, over the stage, and around the walls, the portraits of Philadelphia's great physicians, each President in his day down to Doctor S. Wier Mitchell and noted ones of recent days.

Dr. Redman married Mary Sober in Christ Church. She was one of the belles of the assembly, and her parents among the first subscribers.

The Redmans had two daughters, the elder Sarah, married Daniel Coxe, King's Council, and were the parents of Dr. John Redman Coxe, celebrated in his day as his grandfather was in his.

Dr. Joseph Redman and his father Joseph Redman Esq., were both vestrymen at Christ Church, but Dr. John Redman became an elder in the Second Presbyterian Church, and is buried in the section allotted to that church in Mt. Vernon Cemetery in the same tomb with his wife and daughter Ann and his mother who had been interred fifty years before.

Dr. John besides his greatness as a physician possessed a very beautiful character. In one of the record books in the College of Physicians it is written "His private life was a picture of beauty."

His younger daughter never married and she and her

father and mother lived together in the most perfect love and harmony and died within a few months of each other. The brother Joseph Redman, Esq., was born 1719, and married Elizabeth Parker, daughter of Richard Parker. They had a number of children, John Redman, who married Martha ? ; Dr. Thomas Redman married Sarah Richie, Elizabeth married Col. Elisha Lawrence and Dr. Joseph Redman married Rebecca Turner née Bird. They had two daughters, Elizabeth who married Samuel Ewing 1810, and Maria, Samuel Nicholas, 1814.

All these Redmans were members of Christ Church, and are buried in the same lot in the cemetery at 5th and Arch Sts.

Dr. John Redman adored his elder brother Joseph and when he died in 1779, he delivered a eulogy in which he said that in sixty years there had never been an angry word between them and falling on his knees besought the Lord to comfort and care for his afflicted family.

CHAPTER VIII.
THE ROSS FAMILY.

MANY great men in the early days of this country landed in New Castle, Delaware.
The Rev. George Ross, born in 1679, was the second son of David 2nd of Balblair of Rossshire, Scotland.* Emmanuel Church in New Castle was built for the Rev. George Ross and he lived there until he died in 1754. He was married twice, and had many chidren. George Ross, the signer of the Declaration of Independence, was a son by the second wife, also Gertrude, who married John Reed; Elizabeth, who married Edward Biddle, and Mary Ross, who married Col. Mark Bird of Birdsboro. There were several marriages between the Rosses and the Bird Family. Mark Bird's sister Mary married George Ross, the son of the signer, and they were the parents of nine children. These marriages made the descendants double cousins that created a more intimate feeling of kinship than is usually formed between second and third cousins, athough in the days of our grandmothers and further back, families kept together and visiting at each other's houses was quite the custom. It must have been a little inconvenient at times when an entire family would descend upon a relative without even announcement being made beforehand. The writer remembers when she was a small child visiting an aunt in the South with her mother, when an entire family suddenly arrived in the evening and beds were put up in various places to accommodate the

---

* A Ross had married a daughter of King Robert Bruce and another Ross married his granddaughter.

overflow and yet there was no evidence of annoyance or general discomfort, at least it did not so appear to a little child's mind. Perhaps there were some hidden feelings that were not allowed to come to the surface. Mrs. David Eshleman, of Lancaster, whose husband was leader of the Bar, was a granddaughter of George Ross and Mary Bird, and her son, Mr. Ross Eshleman, has written a genealogy of the Ross family in Lancaster and it is included in the History of the Ross family in Scotland in the Pennsylvania Historical Society.

Our cousin, Miss Mary Ross, who lived for many years with another cousin, Miss Ann Leamy, at 8th and Spruce Streets, was a great-granddaughter of George Ross, the signer, and the last living descendant bearing the name that we know of. After Miss Leamy's death, she went back to Lancaster and ended her days in the home of Mr. Ross Eshleman. Mary Bird, the daughter of Mark Bird, married Daniel Fuller of Lancaster, a lawyer. He was the father of Wm. A. M. Fuller, whose wife was a Miss Wilmer. They had a number of children who are living in Philadelphia and its suburbs. Rebecca Fuller married a Captain Campbell of Virginia, and had two daughters, one of whom survives.

Miss Ann Leamy was that beneficent lady who gave her old homestead to the Episcopal Hospital and in her will left sufficient money to found The Leamy Home at Mt. Airy for Gentlewomen of Philadelphia, who had become reduced in circumstances. The beautiful brick building after the style of an English Manor House with its lovely Italian garden is one of the show places about Philadelphia. Miss Leamy was a granddaughter of John Ross—and a daughter of John Leamy, who came to America, after the Revolutionary War, from Spain, where he had been residing some years and engaged in mercantile business. In

1791 he is noted in Directory as agent for his Catholic Majesty.

For many years he was President of the Marine Insurance Company. He died in 1839, and in his will, made that year, he mentions his wife Elizabeth, and oldest daughter, Ann Leamy, as his heirs.

His portrait is in the book on the Hibernian Society and Friendly Order of St. Patrick among a galaxy of noted Philadelphians.

Betsy Ross.

The Rev. Æneas Ross was a son of the Rev. George Ross of New Castle, and brother to George, the signer. He was Rector of Christ Church for two years, and his son John married Elizabeth Griscom, a member of the church. Her father was one of the three members who were chosen to build Independence Hall. Betsy, as she was nicknamed, must have been a very pretty and attractive girl to have captured an aristocrat. But he seemed contented to get up an upholstery shop with his wife in Arch Street, and when General Washington and George Ross, John's uncle, were looking for some one to make the first flag, it was quite natural to think of Betsy, who had probably the only upholstery shop in the town. She was the wife of a Ross and a member of Christ Church. When John Ross died she married Captain Ashburn, and at his death, John Claypole became her third husband, but she will always be remembered by the name of her first husband. They had one daughter, Margaret, who died at the age of nineteen, unmarried.

When the properties about the little house on Arch Street are bought in, the Park which is to be built around it, will make it one of the very attractive show places of Philadelphia, as it has always been an interesting one.

CHAPTER IX.

JAMES WILSON.

WHEN I saw the first rough draft of the Constitution of the United States written by my great-granduncle I was thrilled. It is now in the Historical Society of Pennsylvania. The Wilson collection is in ten large volumes. Many of the manuscripts were given to the Society by his only granddaughter, Miss Emily Hollingsworth in 1876.

The Constitution is in his firm and beautiful handwriting and the faded and torn blue ribbon with which it was originally tied carefully enclosed between its leaves gave me an extra thrill.

Every great man should have a Boswell and James Wilson is fortunate to have his life written by our Constitutional Historian, Burton Alva Konkle.

We know enough about Mr. Konkle's interpretation of our great men of Colonial days to feel justified in saying there is no one else living who could give this work the sympathetic and scholarly treatment that he has.

Wilson came to this country from Scotland in 1742. He had had a wonderful education at Glasgow, St. Andrews and Edinburgh, under some of the highest lights of Scottish educators.

His parents intended him for the church, but no doubt their disappointment was alleviated in after years when he proved he had chosen the career suited to his mind and talents, as the great jurist, Justice of the Supreme Court and chief maker of the Constitution.

JAMES WILSON, LL.D.

[Reproduction of an oil painting hanging in the Rotunda of the Law School Building of the University. The painting was executed by Albert Rosenthal, from a miniature in the possession of Thomas Harrison Montgomery, Litt.D.]

Washington said, "the convention to frame the Constitution of the United States was made up of the wisest men in America and among the wisest of them was James Wilson."

The enormous collection of letters from the great men of his time, shows how they honored and respected him. Many of these letters are from John Adams, Alexander Hamilton, Patrick Henry, Paul Jones, General St. Clair and Bishop White.

Washington writes, "I experience peculiar pleasure in giving you notice of your appointment to the Office of Associate Judge in the Supreme Court of the United States. Considering the judicial system as the chief pillar upon which our National Government must rest, I have thought it my duty to nominate for the high officers in that department, such men as I conceived would give dignity and lustre to our national character.

"And I flatter myself that the love which you bear to our Country, and the desire to promote general happiness, will lead you to a ready acceptance of the enclosed commission, which is accompanied with such laws as have passed relative to your office.

"I have the honor to be, etc."

Mr. Bronson says, "Pennsylvania had reason to be proud of her adopted son; and throughout our land, so long as that spirit is cherished which gave birth to a Nation designed by God, as we honorably trust, to fulfill a great, noble and glorious mission, shall his name be held in grateful and undying remembrance."

Washington sent his favorite nephew, Bushrod, to study law with him and said, "Tell him we do not only regard him as teacher but as his friend" and later on sends him one hundred guineas as a fee for receiving his nephew in his office as a student of law. When Wilson died, Bushrod succeeded him as Justice of the Supreme Court.

Bishop White and Wilson were devoted friends and the Bishop wrote to Bird Wilson after his father's death that he had been his first friend in America.

When Wilson became very wealthy, General Arthur St. Clair wrote him in 1793, "You are as rich as a jew, but I wish you had ten times as much for you are one that money would not spoil."

Twenty years after he came to this country a cousin in Scotland wrote him, "Do you remember how I persuaded you to let me teach you golf and at the first lesson you beat me, and you have gone on winning all along in America ever since you landed there."

There is such a thrilling description of how Wilson was besieged in his mansion at Third and Walnut Streets, in *Lives of Eminent Philadelphians* that we copy it entirely. His mansion was always afterwards spoken of as Fort Wilson and it was defended by many of the prominent men of the time, aided by the City Troop.

"Perhaps few of those now living can recollect James Wilson in the splendor of his talents and the fullness of his practice. Classically educated and in the outset employed as a tutor in a public seminary, his subsequent success, in a narrow circle of country courts encouraged him to embark in the storm which, after the departure of the British troops, agitated the form of Philadelphia.

The adherents of the royal cause were the necessary subjects of prosecution, and popular prejudice seemed to bar the avenues of justice.

But Wilson never shrunk from such contests; and if his efforts frequently failed, it was not from want of pains or fear of danger. Other questions of the highest moment also became the daily subject of forensic discussion; questions for which previous study no doubt had qualified him, but with which no previous practice had familiarized him. In respect to them, Mr. Wilson soon became conspicuous. The views which he took were luminous and comprehensive. His knowledge and information always appeared adequate to the highest subject and justly administered to the particular aspect in which it was presented. His person and manner were dignified, his voice powerful, though not melodious; his cadences judiciously though somewhat artificially regulated. His discourse was generally of a reasonable length. He did not affect conciseness nor minuteness; he struck at the great features of the case, and neither wearied his hearers by a verbose prolongation, nor disappointed them by an abrupt conclusion. But his manner was rather imposing than persuasive. His habitual effort seemed to be to subdue without conciliating, and the impression left was more like that of submission to a stern than a humane conqueror. In 1773, Mr. Wilson resided on Chestnut Street, between Fourth and Fifth Streets. He afterwards was appointed Justice of the Supreme Court.

Fort Wilson was the name popularly given to a large brick house, formerly on the southwest corner of Walnut and Third Streets. It was in the year 1779 the residence of Mr. Wilson, who became offensive to many for his professional services in behalf of Roberts and Carlisle, men arraigned and executed as tories and traitors. He gave also umbrage from his support of those merchants who refused to regulate their prices by the town resolves. A mob was formed, who gave out an intention to assault his house and injure his person. His friends gathered around him with arms; soon the conflict was joined; many muskets were fired; some were wounded, and a few died. It was a day of great excitement, and long the name and incidents of "Fort Wilson" were discussed and remembered.

Among those in the house were, Messrs Wilson, Morris,

Burd, George and Daniel Clymer, John T. Mifflin, Allen McLane, Sharp Delany, George Campbell, Paul Beck, Thomas Lawrence, Andrew Robinson, John Potts, Samuel C. Morris, Captain Campbell and Generals Mifflin, Nichols and Thompson.

They were provided with arms but their stock of ammunition was very small. While the mob was marching down, General Nichols and Daniel Clymer proceeded hastily to the Arsenal, at Carpenters' Hall and filled their pockets with cartridges, this constituted their whole supply.

In the meantime, the mob and militia (for no regular troops took part in the riot) assembled on the commons, while a meeting of the principal citizens took place at the coffee house. A deputation was sent to endeavor to prevail on them to disperse, but without effect. The first Troop of City Cavalry assembled at their stables, a fixed place of rendezvous, and agreed to have their horses saddled and ready to mount at a moment's warning. Notice was to be given to as many members as could be found and a part was to assemble on Dock below Seventh Street and join the party at the stables. For a time a deceitful calm prevailed. At the dinner hour the members of the Troop retired to their houses and the rebels seized the opportunity to march into the city. The armed men amounted to two hundred, headed by low characters. They marched down Chestnut to Second Street, down Second to Walnut and up Walnut to Mr. Wilson's house with drum beating and two pieces of cannon. They immediately commenced firing on the house, which was warmly returned by the garrison. Finding they could make no impression the mob proceeded to force the door. At the moment it was yielding, the Horse made their appearance. After the Troop had retired at dinner time, hearing that the mob were marching into town, hastened to the rendezvous. These members were, Majors Lennox and the two Nichols, Samuel Morris, Alexander Westbill, Isaac Coxe, and Thomas Leiper.

On their route to Wilson's they were joined by two troopers from Bristol, and turning suddenly round the corner of Chestnut Street, they charged the mob, who ignorant of their number at the cry of "The Horse, the Horse!" dispersed in every direction; but not before two other detachments of the First Troop had reached the scene. Many of them were arrested and committed to prison, and as the sword was very freely used, a considerable number were severely wounded. A man and a boy were killed in the streets; in the house Captain Campbell was killed, and Mr. Mifflin and Mr. Samuel C. Morris wounded. The Troop patrolled the streets the greater part of the night. The citizens turned out, and placed a guard at the powder magazine and the arsenal. It was some days before order was restored. Major Lennox was particularly marked out for destruction. He retired to his house in Germantown; the mob followed and surrounded it during the night, and prepared to force an entrance. Anxious to gain time, he pledged his honor he would open the door as soon as daylight appeared. In the meantime, he contrived to despatch an intrepid woman, who lived in his family to the city for assistance, and a party of the First Troop arrived in season to protect their comrade; but he was compelled to return to town for safety. He was, for a number of years saluted in the market by the title of "Brother Butcher," owing in part to his having been without a coat on the day of the riot, for having on a long coat, he was obliged to cast it aside, to prevent being dragged from his horse. Major Lennox was afterwards upon the death of Thomas Willing, elected President of the First Bank of the United States.

The gentlemen who had comprised the garrison were

advised to leave the city, where their lives were endangered. General and about thirty others accordingly met at Mr. Gray's house below Gray's Ferry, where it was resolved to return to town without any appearance of intimidation. But it was deemed expedient that Mr. Wilson should absent himself for a time. The others continued to walk as usual in public and attended the funeral of the unfortunate Captain Campbell.

Allen McLane and Colonel Grayson got into the house after the fray began. The mob called themselves Constitutionalists. Benezet's fire in the entry from the cellar passage was very effective. Thus ended one of the most famous riots ever known in the annals of Philadelphia.

Mr. Wilson will ever be immortalized as one of the signers of the Declaration of Independence. He died on the 28th of August, 1798, aged fifty-six years."

When Wilson was a struggling lawyer, he fell in love with Rachel Bird, the daughter of William Bird, my great-great-grandfather. He paid court to her for two years and at last in despair of winning her he writes to his great friend Billy (afterwards Bishop William White), who was engaged to Rachel's dear friend, Miss Harrison, and he suggests that she in some subtle way known to women, find out why he cannot persuade her to marry him. As she tells him she enjoys his company, his conversation and his letters, but she cannot think of marriage. Miss Harrison must have been very successful in pleading for the young lawyer who was afterward to become so famous the "Maker of Modern Republics," as his Boswell calls him, for we read that within a year Rachel and James were buying furniture for their home which was afterwards famous also for its luxuriousness and its name, Fort Wilson.

In Rachel's bible are recorded the names of their children:

Mary Wilson, 23 Sep. 1772;
William Wilson, 18 March, 1774;
Bird Wilson, Jan. 18, 1777;
James Wilson, Jr., Nov. 10, 1779;
Emily Wilson, May 11, 1782;
Charles Wilson, Aug.   , 1785.

Mary was the only one of their children who married and she had one daughter who remained single, Miss Emily Hollingsworth.

James Wilson was buried in Christ Churchyard in the same grave with his wife who was Rachel Bird, and the flag flies over their tomb.

Rachel's niece, Elizabeth Redman, married Samuel Ewing.

In 1786, when Wilson was elected a member of the Philosophical Society the Certificate of Membership was signed:

Benjamin Franklin, President,
John Ewing,
William White, Vice-Presidents.

Bird Wilson was born in 1779, and was twenty-one years old when his father passed away in North Carolina, leaving him with two sisters and three young brothers to care for.

But as he was admitted to the bar at this age of twenty-one—the youngest limit allowed by the law—he was soon able to provide a home for his sisters and brothers.

He had graduated at the early age of fifteen and the story of his boyhood by his biographer, W. White Bronson, the grandson of Bishop White, shows what a remarkable child he must have been. His father accorded him the privilege of bringing his books and playthings into his private office as also of being his constant companion even when called upon in consultation upon matters either of public or private business, the details of which were strictly confidential. And even after he had reached an age when communications of such a nature could not possibly have been made without his being a party to the knowledge of them, at least; yet, no objection was ever made to his presence as of one who might ignorantly, heedlessly or wilfully divulge what was never intended to be repeated in the public ear.

The following sketch is copied from *Lives of Eminent Philadelphians*. It is a short and concise account of his career as lawyer, judge, clergyman and Professor of Systematic Divinity in the General Theological Seminary.

"REV. BIRD WILSON, D.D., LL.D.

"The Rev. Bird Wilson, D.D., LL.D., and Emeritus Professor of Systematic Divinity in the General Theological Seminary of the Protestant Episcopal Church, died at his residence in New York City, on the 14th April, 1859, in the eighty-third year of his age. Dr. Wilson was a member of one of the first families in Pennsylvania and in early life embraced the profession of the law, practicing in Norristown, Pennsylvania, and afterwards in Philadelphia. The *New York Courier* says, 'He also was elevated to a seat on the Bench, which he occupied for a time with great credit to himself and for which his legal abilities and acquirements, and great purity of character peculiarly fitted him. Abandoning the profession of the law for that of divinity, he took orders in the Protestant Episcopal Church and was afterwards appointed Professor in the General Theological Seminary in New York City, and at the time of his death had held the position for twenty-nine years. A jurist of professional learning and spotless integrity, a clergyman in whom shone noiselessly but with beautiful distinctness, all the graces of the christian faith, a teacher of divinity with a capability to impart to the student in the happiest manner the rich stores of his ecclesiastical lore, and a man of extraordinary regularity of habit, simplicity of life and guilelessness of heart, Dr. Wilson lived a long life of usefulness, commanding the love and respect of all, and passes to his grave commanding the universal tribute of grief.'"

It is said that Judge Wilson resigned his judgship and became a clergyman because he was not willing to condemn a man to death for the second time. Just before his death, during delirium, he exclaimed with bitterness he "was launched into eternity unprepared, but oh, God, impute it not to me" and when his friend and biographer attempted to sooth and comfort him by reminding him that this happened years ago when he was a judge and that now he was a clergyman he quickly replied, "What of all that? Do you suppose that I am not to answer for what I did as a judge?" This sad scene was witnessed by his beloved niece, Miss Emily Hollingsworth, who had lived with him since the death of her mother and watched over him in his old age and last three years of semi-invalidism.

When they were considering the appointment of an assistant bishop, as Bishop White was growing old and feeble, it is well known his choice was for his beloved friend and pupil in theology, Dr. Wilson, but the project fell through and on his death in 1836, his family at once requested Dr. Wilson be entrusted with the literary remains of the Bishop, and he wrote the memoir which is the history of the establishment of the early Protestant Episcopal Church in America.

When Dr. Wilson passed away in 1859, after services in New York his remains were brought to Philadelphia and placed before the altar in Christ Church until it was carried to its last resting place in Christ Church Cemetery at Fifth and Arch Streets. His tomb is beside his beloved sister, Mary Wilson Hollingsworth.

CHAPTER X.

THE MARY WILSON LETTERS.

THESE letters are in the James Wilson collection at the Historical Society. Much of this collection was given by Miss Emily Hollingsworth just before her death in 1895. She was his only granddaughter and Mary's only child.

When Mary's mother died in 1786, she was only fourteen and the eldest of three boys and one sister, Emily.

Their Aunt Redman was a second mother to them and they grew up with her three daughters, more like brothers and sisters than first cousins. We find in the records of Christ Church they were confirmed the same day, my great-grandmother with them, by Bishop William White, with whose family Mary spent much of her time.

MARCH 23, 1799.

"Confirmed in Christ Church.
"Rebecca Redman,
"Eliza Redman (Elizabeth),
"Maria Redman,
"Mary Wilson,
"Emily Wilson,
"Emily Rush."

In those days the beautiful name of Elizabeth was generally shortened to Eliza which has always seemed a great pity. My grandmother was christened Elizabeth. When James Wilson became involved in the financial debacle after the Revolution, my great-grandmother's home was again open to them and Mary writes much of her Aunt Redman and her "sweet little cousins" as she calls them.

Juliana was married by this time to William Miller. She was near Mary's age and was Mrs. Redman's daughter by her first husband, Peter Turner. Mary's letters were written to her great friend, Sally Chauncey, of New Haven, Conn., daughter of Judge Chauncey, who called Mary his adopted daughter. The letters are filled with her affection for all the family, and as soon as Bird Wilson was able to provide a home Mary constantly urges them to come to her and there are many visits alluded to back and forth between the two families.

It was not easy travelling between New Haven and Philadelphia in those days, but youth and love triumphed over difficulties.

Two of Miss Chauncey's brothers are in Philadelphia and are much with the Wilsons.

There was an early romance between Charles and Mary, and the break throws a cloud over Mary's tender heart for several years. Sally is her confidant and in one letter she rather resents her friend saying she was too proud. Some years later when Charles marries, Mary is as friendly as she had always been after the break between them.

She is so glad to have her own home again and we find her having her Monday evening receptions.

The interesting people of the day came. Many of the Christ Church circle. Among them her devoted friends, the White family, and the Bronsons, the Macphersons, the Montgomerys, the Halls and the Ewings and many others. While my grandmother entertains them with her delightful music, Mary writes her friend, Elizabeth and Maria are wonderful favorites with her brother, Charles. Elizabeth must have loved her cousins very dearly for she named three of her five children after them, among them my father, named after Charles, whose early death was one of Mary's great sorrows. In one place she speaks of her brothers, Bird and Charles, as "two very extraordinary personages."

Of Bird Wilson it was certainly true as a boy and a man and as a lawyer, Judge and clergyman, honored and beloved by everyone. It has been the writer's privilege recently to read his life written by a grandson of Bishop White, the Rev. W. White Bronson, and I have not often been so impressed with the beauty of a human soul.

The desire of Mary's heart was a marriage between her friend, Miss Chauncey, and her brother, Bird, but Mary was doomed to disappointment and Bird never married.

My great grandmother had her summer home in Norristown, and on Walnut Street in winter, very near the Wilson home—not the home of their childhood, Fort Wilson, as it was called—but a modest one provided by Bird, and Mary writes her friend, Aunt Redman has moved into a fine new house farther up Walnut Street and there are many parties given by the Redmans, and she often finds her relations quite worn out with their dissipations. Five parties in one week, one at her Aunt Redman's and Mary attends three out of the five. About this time occurs the death of their sailor brother, James Wilson, Jr. Bird has bought a home on the outskirts of Norristown with 30 acres, in 1807, and although their hearts are bowed with grief, Mary tries to interest herself in Oaklands as it was called. The garden appealed to her, all so different from the city home.

She has only been there three days when her first visitors from Philadelphia arrive, Elizabeth Redman and Samuel Ewing. They were not engaged yet but no doubt were well on the way. It was after the Wilsons had removed to Norristown that Emily died very suddenly. Mary was overcome with her loss, the sister of whom she wrote she possessed all the charm and attraction that she lacked. Bird could never speak of her, his grief was so profound. Missing him one day just before the funeral, they were anxious and searching they found him lying on the bed beside the form of his beloved sister. It was about this time that Elizabeth Redman was married to Samuel Ewing in Christ Church, but we miss all comments by Mary to her friend as it was many months before she could write even to her dear Sally Chauncey. My grandmother must have loved her cousin, Emily, very much for she named her oldest child after her, Emily Wilson, who was afterwards to become such a beauty and married a rector of St. Luke's Church, Philadelphia, the Rev. W. W. Speer, of Charleston, S. C.

After this Mary has no heart for any more gaieties and even her letters show a vein of sadness. When she finally became engaged to Paschall Hollingsworth it is with thanksgiving and relief that we read that at last some happiness was hers, only marred by the thought of leaving her adored brother, Bird. Then follows a trip to Niagara with her fiancé and his father, but as they stop in New Haven the description of the journey is told and not written so we miss her impressions and experiences. But an account of the journey from New Haven is told in the following letter. The Sunday episode is very amusing to us if somewhat annoying to the party. Mary treats the annoyance with her usual courage and serenity.

"OCT. 31, 1811.

"Your good father, my dear Sally, has no doubt been scolding Mary Wilson for not writing. The fact is this is the first day I have attempted to write a letter since my return. After such an absence much must be attended to and we have not been one day until now without company. Still I have not had the business to engross one, I expected when I left you of which I will give you some account presently.

"We had a pretty comfortable journey home until the two last mornings when it rained very much, but yet our anxiety to reach home prevented our stopping, especially as we had been detained a day on the road in consequence of our remaining too long with you and relying on your father's opinion that we should not be 'way laid.' You must tell him Bird owes him a grudge for it. We left Stamford before daybreak, that we might get beyond the line for fear of the worst, when just as we thought ourselves pretty secure and just after sun rise a man for conscience sake flew at the head of the horse and in a violent passion declared we should not travel on the Sabbath and obliged us to return to the nearest tavern to pass the day. I could not forbear telling him I thought he committed a much greater sin by being in a passion on the Sabbath day than we did by riding. That did not soften him, you may be sure. We made the best of it, however, went to church, heard a good sermon and passed a comfortable day.

"About four o'clock the man of authority sent us word as he discovered we were orderly folks, and behaved well in church, we might proceed unmolested. Perhaps my lesson Sally, was of service. The good couple at the tavern, who did everything in their power to make us comfortable told us they had never been without company on that day since the present officer had had authority, though he had never had power before and he loved to exercise it now, and always did it in a passion, and only the week proceeding had obliged a party to pay thirty-nine dollars for endeavoring to elude him.

"We therefore came off very well. Indeed, I believe it was of service to me in more ways than one, as I had never recovered from the fatigue of my ride from Boston to Hartford, and really required a day of rest for my poor body and felt much better after it though did not perfectly recover for several days after we reached home.

"Since then, however, I have really been in more perfect health than I have enjoyed for very many years and, by attention, hope to retain it. About ten days ago I went to town for a few hours and of course saw your good sister. She was far from well, but my brother has just returned from there and says she is very much better, indeed. She and your brother paid him a visit while he was holding court in Chester and they have promised to come up here on Saturday should the weather be favorable. Now my dear Sally, for my own particular concerns, when I left you I expected to be very much engaged, but owing to the difficulties of the commercial world, we have judged it most convenient to defer it for a few months; not that the business of my friend and his father has been in the least afflicted but it would inconvenience the old gentleman to draw a sufficient sum for the house just at present to make the necessary arrangements. I therefore feel as if I was tranquilly fixed for the winter in still contributing to my good brother's comfort. I give you these particulars for the satisfaction of your family alone. When questioned on the subject, you may just reply circumstances make it convenient to defer it for some time.

"I have nothing interesting to communicate, my dear Sally. I found everybody and everything in status quo on my return and they have remained so since, except that I am quite deserted even by Catherine Bird who has gone agadding to town. I found my dear Rebecca here and she remained with me until yesterday when she went with

Aunt Redman and Juliana Miller, who have left Norris for the winter. Bird goes again on Sunday for a fortnight and leaves me quite solitary, but I shall manage very well with my books, which have been so long neglected and a never feeling resource to us females. You must write to enliven my solitude and tell me everything respecting each member of your family circle that will interest me. If I had wings, even seven league boots, I would let the house take care of itself and pay you frequent visits, when deserted in this manner. But as it is I must begin to accommodate myself to stationary habits, for as I trust I shall no longer have the plea of ill health to second my inclination to visit my distant friends, they will, notwithstanding live in my most affectionate remembrance and I hope I will not be entirely forgotten by them. Present me most respectfully to your dear parents. Tell your dear father I delivered all his messages to the frenchman who would be grateful for his advice as he thinks he should fare better for it. For yourself, Abby and Nathaniel accept much affection from your

"MARY WILSON.
"Bird unites in affection to you all."

The putting off of the marriage for several months, Mary accepts with her usual good sense and finds her compensation in remaining longer with her beloved brother. She must have had her heart torn in two, but marriage in those days was far more important than in these days of woman's independence and emancipation and the mania for employment in every line.

Mary's Aunt Redman is greatly relieved for she tells her she could not bear to have one of her nieces die an old maid.

"OAKLAND, Jan. 26, 1812.

"Soon after the receipt of your last, my dear Sally, I went to town, so deferred answering it until my return, in hopes of gaining some material for a letter. I exercise my faculties in that way so seldom I really am under the necessity of relying pretty much on outward circumstances to furnish one. I went to the city in high spirits anticipating much enjoyment from the society of many friends, who were too much hampered to come to me. For a fortnight my expectations were fully realized. After that I caught a severe cold for which our old friend, Dr. Rush, bled me and confined me to the house on 'bread and water' as Aunt Redman says. The first time I ventured out was to get into the gig to be conveyed home, where I have now been about a fortnight and only once outside of the door from some remains of my cold but more for the extremity of the weather, which for its continuance exceeds anything we have hereto experienced for years. We have passed our time, notwithstanding, most comfortably.

"Rebecca Lawrence, Cousin Kate and myself (Bird being absent) form a most agreeable trio and have accomplished abundance of work and reading and are so much pleased with each other or with a good hickory fire we seldom separate until the midnight hour is fast approaching. To-morrow we expect our circle will be enlarged by my good brother's return and a visit from *my friend* accompanied by a very charming girl, Mary Fox, the daughter of the late Samuel Fox, of whom no doubt you have heard your brother speak. The family spent last summer in Norris. We all became so sociable, the two elder young ladies promised a visit each in the course of the winter. Mary was to have come up last Saturday, but was prevented. She will be quite an acquisition to our little circle. She is very sprightly and conversable and with all very beautiful. They laugh and say Bird must guard well his heart. I assure you we do not often meet so sweet a girl. My intention was to tell you all about the city before beginning on home affairs, but I suppose 'nearest the heart nearest the pen,' as well as 'nearest the tongue.'

"I dined twice at your good brother's and was really rejoiced to observe the great change in your dear sister; she was under the effect of a bad cold at the time and yet was so evidently improved in strength and appearance I was astonished. I met Dr. Physick there: 'This is a very different lady from the one you and I used to consult so anxiously about last winter, Miss Wilson.' So you see his opinion. He rarely calls more than once a fortnight and then only, as he says, that she may not forget him.

"I saw many more of your friends who were all well. Among others, Mrs. Ralston and her daughter; report says Rebecca is engaged to James Montgomery, though with what foundation, I know not; I heard nothing of it at your brother's. I am glad you found the society of Mrs. Day an acquisition. If any congeniality exist between her and her husband it must be so, and that there does I fervently hope for the sake of so truly estimable a being.

"You say nothing of the other newly married couple, Mr. Kingsley and his wife. Have you not made an acquaintance with her? Or, knowing my high consideration for the other professor have been induced to meet him and her? Well, I am quite satisfied with such a reason.

"You have probably been looking for this for some time. The fact is, my dear Sally, my pen and my fingers feel a stronger antipathy to each other than ever, but one short letter have I written since the receipt of yours and this I was able to write.

"However, you have no great reason to complain. Seven

weeks had elapsed ere I received an answer to my last, but this is not retaliation; unfortunately it is the genuine spirit of procrastination which has run in my veins since I first put pen to paper and will so continue to do, I fear, to the end of the chapter. Even should Dr. Rush cause them to flow to the life itself, it governs my fingers but not my thoughts and in them, my dear, dear Sally, you and your respected parents and sister always hold an affectionate station. Tell your dear father I regret he does not approve 'putting off'; in the present case, however, I trust it will prove for the best and as it will allow him more time, I hope for a longer letter when occasion does call for it. Present me affectionately to both parents and Abby and believe me ever yours,

"MARY.

"How is poor Mrs. D. and her still poorer invalids this hard season? I enclose a mite for her from a sum I had appropriated to preparation for an event that increasing my own comforts will not, I trust, render me more insensible to the want of it in others. I leave to your discretion either to give to her or to procure what will best answer my object to contribute to her comfort."

This is the last letter we have until after her marriage and removal to Philadelphia.

The Rebecca Lawrence mentioned as one of the trio "enjoying the books and work around the hickory fire" was the daughter of Colonel Elisha Lawrence, who married Elizabeth Redman, a sister of Mary's uncle, Dr. Joseph Redman, the writer's great-grandfather. "Cousin Kate" is Catherine Bird who spent much time with Mary, the daughter of Mark Bird and Mary Ross, the sister of George Ross, the signer.

"PHILA., Oct. 19, 1812.

"It is frequently the case, my dear Sally, I must commence my letters by apologizing for having deferred sending one so long, but when I assure you I have written but one since I last wrote to yourself, and that to my dear brother, you will, I am convinced, forgive one. You have often been the subject of my thoughts and wishes and your dear family, for the last fortnight, of my anxiety.

"Your invaluable mother's illness was not known to me sooner. I had had a cold which prevented my seeing your brother or sister during the most serious period of her indisposition. My intention was to have written immediately but our house has been full of company and some of them being strangers I felt obliged to devote much of my time to them.

"Some of them are still with us; among them for a few days was our favorite Patty Hall. She left me Friday evening to return to Mary Bronson and talks of returning to Baltimore in the course of a week. She is quite well and would no doubt have much for me to communicate did she know I was writing.

"The moment I heard of the arrival of Charlotte Chester I went round, when the favorable accounts she gave me of your dear Mama entirely released my anxiety. Say everything affectionate and respectful for me to her. She must not forget her Mary who will ever continue to love her as a daughter.

"As to your good father, I fear he begins to forget me. He not only refused to be present when I was married, although the only person I wished to be present, except my brother and Mrs. Macpherson, but has never sent me the letter of advice he kindly promised me. I still wish it though I have ceased to expect it.

"The last summer proved a most trying one to me. Your letter found me on the bed of sickness with a violent rheumatism in every part of my frame that reduced me so low that my friends entertained but feeble hopes of my recovery.

"I am now in better health than I have enjoyed for years though I feel I must be careful of myself the ensuing winter. No scenes of gaiety do I wish to engage in; my avoiding them, therefore, will prove no sacrifice, but rather add to the enjoyment of the society of my friends. How much I wish, my dear Sally, you were to pass this winter in Philadelphia. There is a possibility Patty may return in the course of it when we should make such a sociable circle. Mary Bronson has another daughter but still she does not nurse it herself. I expect we should be frequently together. Betsy Macpherson comes in to pass the day with me every now and then. The General is in a most melancholy situation; the tumor has spread half over his face and has deprived him of the use of one of his eyes and almost at times of his articulation. His paroxisms are so violent there is no counting a day on his existence. Before your Mama's illness, Mrs. Chauncey told me Abby would pass the winter here. I hope that being removed she still intends it. I shall not say a word as to the portion of time I shall lay claim to until her arrival when I shall place before her all the whys and wherefores and take no denial. She must recollect she is a great favorite of Mr. Hollingsworth who will also put in his demands.

"I have no news for you. We hear nothing but politics and they are of the most gloomy cast. I often wish we were inhabitants of dear Connecticut and then we should feel a respect for our State.

"Remember me with affection to all those who still inquire for me and particularly to Clara Darling. Let me know what her situation is at present.

"I must now bid you adieu. I have two letters to write which I can no longer in conscience defer, one to poor Alice Babcock, to whom I have not written since last winter and who has met with very severe trials lately, the failure of her husband, the loss of an infant and the removal from her friends into the country. So, my good girl, you see you only share the effects of my dislike to my pen. My affection you largely share.

"M. HOLLINGSWORTH."

Mary's two friends, Betsy Macpherson and Mary Bronson, were the two married daughters of Bishop White, and they had always been intimate as their fathers were before them.

"PHILA., Dec. 27, 1818.

"Writing is not a usual Sunday occupation with me, my beloved Sally, but we are instructed to visit the house of mourning to make the heart better. When debarred from that, will not expressing feelings of sympathy and endeavoring to raise the mind to the only source of comfort and consolation under very trying dispensations also have some beneficial effect on the heart? I trust so, particularly feelings so sincerely participating in the bereavement you have just experienced. When the intelligence of the situation of your mother first reached me I was greatly shocked, but the moment reflection returned I wept for her survivors, though not for her, since, my dear Sally, I have frequently thought that could I feel as entire confidence in a preparation for Heaven of any human being while in the full exercise of the duties of this life, it was of the being whose translation to a state of blessedness we now contemplate.

"With such a reparation, even in the awful act of dissolution, she has been blessed. The sweet serenity that appeared on her countenance proved the absence of suffering and she was also exempted from witnessing that of her afflicted family. O, my friend, may we lead the life of piety she did, then will death and the grave be robbed of their sting and victory.

"Tell your dear surviving parent that through the whole of last week I felt more than normally his daughter. How much did I wish I could be with you, sharing in your cares, anxieties and endeavors to administer all the comforts we could to his agonized spirit. His being surrounded by all his children, save one, at such a moment must have been a source of great comfort to him (poor Elihu, how keen his suffering). In his most trying visitations the Father of all Goodness remembers mercy.

"To my dear affectionate Abby, what can I say that her own good sense has not already suggested? Dear girl, so diffident of your own powers, how severely are you called upon to exert every faculty of your soul to sooth the declining years of your afflicted father. May your Heavenly Father support and strengthen you under your present acute feelings. How much I love and symathize with you at this time. I long to hear just how you all are. I hope I shall by the return of your brother. I spent one hour at his house on Christmas evening, the only time I have been out for three weeks; have been much indisposed. At present I cannot go, having as yet no appropriate dress. I shall go the first moment I can. My dear Nathaniel, I understand, remains some time with you. Remember me most particularly to him.

"Dear, dear Sally, do write the moment your feelings and leisure will permit, if but a line; you know not how anxiously it will be looked for by

"Your sincerely affectionate
"M. HOLLINGSWORTH.
"To Mr. Woolsey, present me with affectionate respect."

"To Mrs. William Woolsey, c/o Judge Chauncey, New Haven.

"As George precedes my brother and myself, it gives me an opportunity, my dear friend, of saying I promise myself the pleasure of being with you on Tuesday evening, should the weather prove favorable the morning of the day, if not, on the first clear day. I can with difficulty realize, my beloved Sally, I shall once more be under the roof of one with whom I have passed some of the happiest days, I may say months, of my life. Though again induced to incur obligations that I fear must ever remain unrequitted, but I feel I know you too well to pain you by dwelling on that point and will only assure you my determination is, it shall not interfere with my promised enjoyment.

"With best respects to Mr. Woolsey and regards to my dear Sarah, believe me

"Ever yours,
"M. HOLLINGSWORTH.
"To Mrs. Woolsey, Greenwich St., New York."

This little note without date is the last of Mary Wilson's in the collection and it makes us want to know more, particularly of the married life of the two friends. They are not brilliant letters in any way, but they tell the domestic and social story of a fine gentlewoman of the time when

Christ Church was the center of so many old cultured families. Many names that give us a thrill, when we read of the patriotism and sincere and loyal devotion, not only to their country, but to each other. Hospitality had not gone out of fashion and families held together and friendship was not only a name. Life was not the mad and exciting whirl it is today and it has been refreshing to read of the house parties, round the wood fires, with their reading and their work. If Mary Wilson was not noted in any remarkable way, as her father and her brother, we must accord her one great virtue; she was the perfect friend and perhaps that is the rarest thing in this old world where often it seems as if it did not exist. Emerson says, "Our friendships hurry to short and poor conclusions, because we have made them a texture of wine and dreams instead of the tough fibre of the human heart. We snatch at the slowest fruit in the whole garden of God, which many summers and many winters must ripen."

We gather this one lesson of friendship from the letters as well as many charming things that make them quite worth our while to spend some quiet hours with.

The collection of letters has one at the end written years after, in 1849, by Mary's daughter and James Wilson's only grandchild, Emily Hollingsworth, to her Uncle Bird, with whom she lived until his death in 1859. She was his only heir and one of her first acts after his death was to erect a neat and beautiful chapel at the Episcopal Hospital as a memorial to his memory. The Episcopal Hospital had been the homestead of our cousin, Miss Ann Leamy, and she had bequeathed it as also sufficient money to found the Leamy Home at Mt. Airy.

The fine and beautiful character of Miss Emily Hollingsworth is well known to many who are living today. She spent much time reading to the sick in the hospitals and to the writer, whose privilege it was to see her a number of times, she seemed to be the personification of goodness and mercy. After her uncle's death she made her home at the house of her cousin, Dr. Caspar Morris, in Philadelphia. She died in 1895.

"G*reenhill*, Wed. 20, 1847.

"M*y* V*ery* D*ear* U*ncle*:—

"Thank you for the kind indulgences, expressed towards me in the letter I received from you yesterday afternoon. I really believe I am deriving benefit from the pure air here and wish to return to you dear uncle 'well and cheerful,' therefore, deem it best to prolong my visit among my kind friends until circumstances point to a suitable time to return. Be assured, however, I shall not be unmindful of the kind feelings and the wish to have me with you, that you express so generously towards me. I am afraid this letter will not reach you before the end of the week as I think there will be no opportunity to send it in tomorrow and being Meeting day, uncle seldom goes into the city. At any time if you do not receive my letters regularly, please attribute it to my distance from the city. Papa is now here on a visit. He desires affectionate remembrance to you and requests me to enclose the copy of his letter to Mr. Loeser which you had asked him to write as, under the new regulation of the Post Office, it will not increase the postage of the letter.

"Cousin Henry went to Pottsville week before last and saw Mr. Loeser, who said he had received my father's letter but had not answered it. I am sorry to learn that cousin Hetty Harris was so unwell. From what Mary Montgomery tells me it is probably Elizabeth Willbank's situation pressed much on Hetty's mind, besides the devoted attention she was able to pay to Dr. Harris during his illness last winter has had the effect of exhausting her frame. Mary says she looked worn out when she was in Philadelphia. You have probably been informed of the arrangements made for Elizabeth and Mr. Willbank. The last I heard of her she was still at Mary Montgomery's but I have not been in town for nearly two weeks, there being nothing to call me to the city. From this cause I know nothing of our Philadelphia friends, but of this family circle. We are going on very pleasantly here, walking and reading with occasional rides.

"The country looks unusually green and bright, having been refreshed by almost daily showers. Uncle reports an abundance of peaches on the market; he heard of some being sold that were a little bruised for $12\frac{1}{2}$ cts. the basket. I hope the supply has reached you in plenty. Much love to Nanny. I am very glad to hear she is coming on nicely and I shall be happy to receive her letter when entirely convenient to her to write it. Love to Tommy and also the girls in 19th Street.

"I regret to learn of Marion's detention and the cause of it. Tell Alice I intend soon to write her a letter and am glad she has returned home well and trust after a pleasant visit. Probably Aunt Miller will have left you before this letter arrives. If her stay has been prolonged, however, remember me affectionately to her. Kind regards to George and Lucy. As it is time to dress for tea, I will now bid my dear uncle farewell for the present.

"Your affectionate child,
"EMILY HOLLINGSWORTH."

CHAPTER XI.

THE CHILDREN OF SAMUEL EWING AND ELIZABETH REDMAN.

Emily Wilson   Juliana
   Ellen   Mary
         and
     Charles Henry

EMILY WILSON was named for her famous great-uncle, James Wilson, and his lovely daughter, Emily, whose death at Norristown was such a grief to Bird and Mary Wilson. Emily Ewing, like her cousin, was a lovely person and a beauty.

Only fourteen when her father died in 1825, she was the rock on which her family leaned. An Assembly beau wrote a poem on twenty of the debutantes of the day. I only remember the two lines as it was read to me when a child by my uncle who was so proud of his beautiful wife:—

"Young men, beware, or it will prove your undoing
If you gaze too long upon Emily Ewing."

Dr. William W. Speer was from South Carolina and Rector of St. Luke's Church in this city. As an old man I have often heard him tell the story of his courtship in the gardens of the Woodland, which was then a family estate and rented for the summer by some of our relations.

Dr. Speer was a very tall and handsome man, but my grandmother had ambitions for her beautiful daughter, and the clergyman was denied. But love triumphed, and Aunt Emily became his wife. As she was the oldest and my father the youngest, and I the youngest of my father's family, my aunt was an old lady before I saw her, but I shall never forget her gracious manner, her beautiful hands and neck, around which she always wore soft, beautiful laces. Today she would still be a beauty, even after middle age. But in her time, alas! Did not Madame de Genlis say at thirty "she retired from the world and left off rouge"?

Many of the family who wandered through the garden of the Woodlands are buried there now. My grandmother, the Goddards, the Elberts, the Nicholases, the Mitchells and many others.

The last time I was in the old yellow mansion the superintendent told me of a secret stairway from a concealed panel on the second floor from which a bride and groom disappeared mysteriously after the wedding and so escaped the storm of rice and slippers while the guests were waiting at the foot of the grand stairway. It quite thrilled me that such a thing could exist in quiet, old Philadelphia. It isn't quiet any more.

Julia, the third daughter of Samuel Ewing, was named after her mother's half-sister Juliana Miller, neé Turner. The family always said she had been a handsome girl and my first remembrance of her was that she was very vivacious and witty and possessed a beautiful nose, which, I think, is a great asset for beauty. Mary Cholmondely says, in one of her well-known novels, "Eyes grow dim and teeth decay, but a beautiful nose is a resting place for one's vanity."

Julia married John Grimké Drayton, of Charleston, South Carolina, who had inherited the estate next to Drayton Hall, Magnolia Gardens on the Ashley. That Earthly Paradise was the result of his untiring devotion and genius.

Paul Frost, in *The House Beautiful* for August, 1923, writes an article: "Magnolia and its Significance, a key that has unlocked a secret to vast resources."

He says "Magnolia would be called the fairest garden in America or Europe did it not stand absolutely by itself, incomparable and indescribable For those, the least sensitive, the first view is overwhelming; to the very sensitive, it is almost an overpowering thing. It nearly goes to the head. One has to steady oneself."

A few years ago Elmendorf, at the Academy of Music, Philadelphia, in an illustrated lecture on Charleston, said he had been all over the world, but had never seen such unearthly beauty as at Magnolia on the Ashley, and John Galsworthy, who spent some time there recently, laid the scene of a story in the gardens, and calls them the most beautiful spot on earth. The Hedonist was published in the July *Century,* 1922.

The following leaflet is given to the tourists who visit Magnolia every day in the season.

A SHORT HISTORY AND DESCRIPTION OF THE FAMOUS
"MAGNOLIA GARDENS"
Near Charleston, S. C.

(This estate is conceded by competent judges to be the most beautiful garden in the world.)

For about two hundred and twenty-five years the estate named "Magnolia-on-the-Ashley", but now better known to the public as "Magnolia Gardens", has continuously been owned by the Drayton family and their descendants. The colonial mansion of brick was destroyed by fire in the revolutionary period, and a second dwelling was burned during the war between the States.

The old steps of this second residence now lead up to the present cottage—the springtime residence of the owner. A short time after inheriting this plantation, then comprising 1872 acres, the Reverend John Grimké Drayton, owing to failing health, was ordered by his physician to spend his life in the open air. He conceived the idea of creating a garden, and thus was commenced the wonderland whose unrivalled beauty to-day is a monument to his exquisite taste and rare poetic feelings. The first plants of the species known as "Azalea Indica" were planted by Mr. Drayton in 1843. These plants were imported into this country from the Orient to Philadelphia, Pa. The climate of Pennsylvania proved to be too severe for them, and Mr. Drayton was requested to try them in South Carolina. The garden comprising 16 acres reveals the success of the experiment. In addition to the immense collection of azaleas, there is a very valuable collection of the "Camellia Japonica." Probably nowhere else may be found as many different varieties of these beautiful plants and flowers.

The Camellias bloom somewhat earlier than the azaleas, so that tourists rarely see them in great profusion. This estate took its name from its many fine specimens of the "Magnolia Grandiflora." In early May the bloom of these trees adds an aftermath of loveliness to the garden. Among many other interesting trees and shrubs there is a specimen of the California Redwood. The parent tree was blown down in a cyclone, and the present tree is one of its branches, having sprung up from the recumbent trunk.

When Phosphate Rock was discovered, Mr. Drayton sold most of his acreage to mining companies. There are heavy deposits of this rock underlying the garden and lawn.

In front of the present residence, skirted by magnificent

live oaks planted when the estate was young—a marked contrast to the exotic bloom and riot of color of the garden—lies the lawn,—the English-like dignity of which is a restful feature. This lawn is traversed by an avenue of live oaks equal in stateliness to itself. The garden has never felt the touch of a professional landscape architect, for upon the death of Mr. Drayton in 1891 the care of it was assumed by his granddaughter, who inherited his love of, and skill with flowers. The direction of the garden is still in her hands, and only as a result of her unceasing attention has the standard set by Mr. Drayton been maintained. When Mr. Drayton passed away, the property was inherited by his eldest daughter, Julia Drayton, wife of the late Wm. S. Hastie of Charleston. Mrs. Hastie died in 1920 leaving Magnolia to her only surviving son C. Norwood Hastie.

Many descriptions of Magnolia have been written from time to time. From among the number the following are reprinted.

The following description of these gardens, by Miss Constance Fenimore Woolson, appeared in *Harper's Magazine* of December, 1875.

"The Glory of the Gardens

is the gorgeous coloring of the azaleas. Some of the bushes are twenty feet through and fifteen feet high—solid masses of blossoms in all shades of red from palest pink to deepest crimson, from lilac-blue to deepest purple, and now and then a pure white bush like a bride in her snowy lace. It is almost impossible to give the stranger an idea of the affluence of color in this garden when its flowers are in bloom. Imagine long walks with the moss-draped live oaks overhead, a fairy lake and bridge in the distance, and on each side the great masses of rose and pink and crimson, reaching far above your head, thousands upon tens of thousands of blossoms packed close together, with no green to mar the density of their color, rounded out in swelling curves of bloom, down to the turf below, not pausing a few inches above it, and showing bare stems or trunk, but spreading over the velvet and trailing out like the rich robes of an Empress. Stand on one side and look across the lawn, it is like a mad artist's dream of hues—it is like the Arabian Nights, eyes that have never had color enough find here a full feast and go away satisfied at last. And with all their gorgeousness the hues are delicately mingled, the magic effect produced, not by unbroken banks of crude reds, but by blended shades like the rich Oriental patterns of India shawls, which the European designers, with all their efforts, can never imitate. Sometimes in Northern gardens one sees carefully tended a little bed of scarlet geraniums, all in bloom, or else a mound of verbenas in various shades. Imagine these twelve or thirteen feet high, extending in long vistas in all directions as far as the eye can reach, and you have a faint idea of the beautiful Spring Gardens of Magnolia-on-the-Ashley."

More than twenty years afterwards, *The News and Courier,* of Charleston, said:

"Far up the Ashley, where the waters from the Atlantic only ebb and flow languorously, where either bank is lined for miles with the greenest marsh grass, overhung by great moss-draped oaks, there is a garden spot so lovely it seems to have been dropped from a fairy tale. It is like the storied gardens, with beautifully kept walks, rustic bridges over placid waters, a canopy of silver-gray moss suspended from wide-spreading oaks, a carpet of green velvet shot with violets—and all around are walls of flowers. Here is a huge snow bank of white azaleas, and at its edge, dripping over against it like a blood-red fountain, another great mass of flowers; its neighbor, in turn, a shade paler, and further and further on more and more exquisite banks of blooms. Here and there a giant Camellia japonica tree raises its limbs, covered with smooth, dark green leaves and wax-like flowers—red, mottled and white. Another turn in the path and a beautiful rhododendron comes in view, and over against the cottage, near the middle of the gardens, is a blaze of golden banksias. There are dozens of walks and acres upon acres of flowers. The eyes are filled with color and grace, the senses caressed by the intoxicating perfume from millions of fragrant flower cups. It is a sight worth travelling many miles to see."

From Lady Baltimore—Owen Wister (1905).

"I shall not attempt to describe the azaleas at Live Oaks, (Magnolia Gardens). You will understand me quite well, I am sure, when I say that I had heard the people at Mrs. Trevise's house talk so much about them, and praise them so superlatively, that I was not prepared for much: my experience of life had already included quite a number of azaleas. I have seen gardens, many gardens, in England, in France, in Italy; I have seen what can be done in great hothouses, and on great terraces; what can be done under a roof, and what can be done in the open air with the aid of architecture and sculpture, and ornamental land and water; but no horticulture that I have seen devised by mortal man approaches the unearthly enchantment of the azaleas at Live Oaks. It was not like seeing flowers at all; it was as if there, in the heart of the wild and mystic wood, in the gray gloom of those trees veiled and muffled in their long webs and skeins of hanging moss, a great, magic flame of rose and red and white burned steadily. You looked to see it vanish; you could not imagine that such a thing would stay. All idea of individual petals or species was swept away in this glowing maze of splendor, this transparent labyrinth of rose and red and white, through which you looked beyond, into the gray gloom of the hanging moss and the depths of the wild forest trees. I turned back as often as I could, and to the last caught glimpses of it, burning, glowing and shining like some miracle, some rainbow exorcism, with its flooding fumes of orange-rose and red and white merging magically."

John Galsworthy in the July, 1921, "Century" Magazine

"Everyone who goes to Charleston in the spring soon or late visits Magnolia Gardens. A painter of flowers and trees, I specialize in gardens, and freely assert that none in the world is so beautiful as this. Even before the magnolias come out, it consigns the Boboli at Florence, the Cinnamon Gardens of Colombo, Conception at Malaga, Versailles, Hampton Court, the Generaliffe at Granada, and the La Mortala to the Category of 'also ran.'

"Nothing so free and gracious, so lovely and wistful, nothing so richly colored, yet so ghostlike, exists, planted by the sons of men. It is a kind of paradise which has wandered down, a miraculously enchanted wilderness.

"Brilliant with azaleas, or magnolias, it centers around a pool of dreamy water, overhung by tall trunks wanly festooned with the gray Florida moss. Beyond anything I have ever seen, it is other worldly. And I went there day after day, drawn as one is drawn in youth by visions of the Ionian Sea, of the East, or the Pacific Isles. I used to sit paralyzed by the absurdity of putting brush to canvas in front of that dream pool. I wanted to paint of it a picture like that of the fountain by Helleu, which hangs in the Luxembourg. But I knew I never should." And again he says, "It's perfect. This is the most beautiful spot in the world."

Almost every year Mrs. Drayton would leave her Paradise and come to Philadelphia for long visits with her sister, Mrs. Goddard. She loved the city of her birth and to visit her relatives and friends of her girlhood days, especially those of the Christ Church Circle where her mother's family had been associated for generations. Her father died when she was ten years old and none of his children ever knew their distinguished grandfather, Dr. John Ewing, for his son Samuel was married in Christ Church in 1810, eight years after his father's death in 1802.

The Draytons spent their winters in Charleston, the spring at Magnolia and their summers at Flat Rock, North Carolina. Drayton Hall, adjoining Magnolia, is now a museum.

My uncle Drayton was such a beautiful and interesting character. He was adored by all his wife's family and his rare visits to Philadelphia were much appreciated by them. When he died his oldest daughter inherited Magnolia.

NOTE:—The Camellia Japonicas are in bloom from early February to about the middle of March. The Azalea Indicas generally reaches the height of profusion about the 10th of April, but are very beautiful from the end of March through April.

Inasmuch as the owner of these gardens opens them each spring to the public chiefly to afford pleasure to the flower lovers, many of whom come to Charleston from distant points solely to view them, he requests and expects visitors to refrain from committing any act which might prove detrimental to the garden's appearance. They are urged to bear in mind that *damage to flowers, plants and shrubbery cannot be restored or remedied or even figured in dollars and cents.* For reasons given above the picking of flowers, disturbance of plants, the breaking of shrubbery and lunching on these grounds are strictly prohibited, and will be rigidly enforced.

She married Mr. William Hastie of Charleston. She passed away in 1922, and her daughter manages the wonderful gardens with loving care and efficiency.

My Philadelphia Aunt.

Ellen Ewing, the second child of Samuel Ewing, married John Lacy Goddard, a banker, grandson of Paul Beck and brother of Dr. Paul Goddard.

She represented the type as I first remember her, of a middle aged Philadelphia gentlewoman more than any person I have ever known.

Having no children and married to a whole souled warm hearted man who had a great fondness for all his wife's relations, their greatest pleasure was to keep open house. It was really a second home for all her family. Her sister Mary lived with her until her death in 1856. She was named after Mary Wilson, her mother's beloved cousin

I have heard much of my Aunt Mary's gentleness and kindly spirit and her early death must have been a great grief to her family.

Mrs. Goddard was not a beauty, but her soft dark eyes and beautiful manner I shall never forget. But as I only saw her when she was middle aged I am not capable of judging, and middle age with its mature caps seems very ancient to a child. They spent their summers in West Philadelphia, no doubt quite like the country in those days. Shrub Cottage was on the corner of 39th and Walnut Streets, but after they sold it to my uncle's intimate friend Anthony Drexel, they moved to a charming cottage across the street. Shrub Cottage soon became the handsome home of the Drexels and later the Goddards moved to Locust Street where my aunt spent her long years of widowhood.

John Goddard had been a prominent member of the

Church of the Saviour and St. Mary's on Locust Street, and followed in the footsteps of his father John Goddard who had done much in building up St. Stephen's Church at 10th and Chestnut.

When my uncle died, being grand master of the Masons, my aunt always averse to anything like publicity objected to any demonstration at her quiet home. But the Masons came, several hundred of them, and viewed the casket, passing in and out quietly and my aunt, in her room of mourning, never knew.

The executor, who was a Mason, had taken the responsibility of her displeasure. She never ceased to mourn her husband's death and was never known to make a visit after it. She lived in a quiet stately way retaining the same old servants and keeping her house open for her relatives to come when it pleased them for long visits.

She never changed her style of dress and wore the same dainty little caps. When her dress and cap makers failed or went out of business her friends found others who were willing to go back to the ancient style to please her. It must have been difficult even in those days. Her friends never neglected her and on pleasant days the grand dames of Philadelphia would gather in the Locust Street house and all the genteel gossip of the city was discussed. People often said: "If you want to hear the news go and see Mrs. Goddard, she knows everything about everybody." And of course everybody meant the old circle she had been born and brought up in. Of all her friends Mrs. Edward Shaw seemed to me the most beloved. Her beautiful voice and manner captivated my childish soul also. Then there was her daughter Meta, who married Walter McMichael, who never forgot her mother's dear friend and was such a comfort to my aunt in her old age when so many of the older time had passed on. Mrs. Dr. Paul Goddard was another much beloved and, who could help loving her? She outlived them all and walked down Chestnut Street every morning for her constitutional when she was well over ninety years, and looking not more than sixty with her straight back and steady walk. I always called her Aunt Louisa and loved to go and see her. She had such a sense of humor, and the visits were always gay with laughter and the dear lady in her nineties. She had been one of the beautiful Bonsall girls, famous in their day. Mrs. William Welsh was another old friend who had been my aunt's bridesmaid. They had been next door neighbours, and had grown up together, and were connected through the Ross family, as Mrs. Welsh's mother was Elizabeth Ross.

The Locust Street house had a long garden back, with many fruit trees and berry bushes. They were the delight of the little nieces and the delight also of neighbour's nieces and children in many nocturnal visits. My aunt rather scorned the fruit. They were not the peaches of yesterday. We wondered how they could be better, but youth is not so critical and today I understand. I wonder also, where are the peaches of yesterday? Those old West Philadelphia houses were lovely with their gardens and the streets overhung with wonderfully beautiful trees. It is sad to see the changes that are being made. I hope they will spare the trees along the side walks, even if the gardens have to go. I like to think about my Philadelphia aunt and her old time ways, her dignity and refinement and poise and kindness, and thoughtfulness towards all connected with her by the ties of blood and friendship: Compared with the mad rush and vulgar excitement of today it is refreshing to look back.

But as a child, it was not so much appreciated. Any

marked interest in children that were not within the charmed circle of old families was gently reproved and then that old Philadelphia custom of three o'clock dinner.

We, her frequent guests had our nine o'clock breakfast in the dining room, and exactly at 10 A. M. a little silver bell would tinkle in the upper hall and her breakfast would be taken up to her cosy sitting room where she would discuss with the cook, who lived with her forty years, the requirements for the day in the culinary department. We could go in and bid her good morning, but on finishing her breakfast, she would retire to her boudoir until noon when she would return to her couch in the sitting room with her books and paper and some light sewing or knitting and be ready to welcome the visitors who came from town or the house guests. Her sister Julia, Mrs. John G. Drayton, of Charleston, S. C., who lived in that world paradise Magnolia Gardens, usually spent several months with her sister and revived a little of the life and gaiety of former years. She was very witty and my sister has often told the story of how she, about one o'clock, timorously remarked on being very hungry, our Aunt Julia with a twinkle in her eye replied, "Child, aristocratic stomachs never get hungry before 3 o'clock."

To be sure there were surreptitious visits to the kitchen, and the dear old cook was noted for her biscuits and quince jelly made from the really wonderful quince tree in the garden. Mrs. Goddard was a semi-invalid for several years before her death. She lived her quiet life to a good old age and survived all her family. She sadly missed the visits of her sister, Mrs. Drayton, and her only brother.

She had some odd experiences even in her quiet last days. She had always been timid and never failed to have the maid look under her bed before retiring. This was known and caused much amusement among her relatives and friends. One night the maid glanced as usual, and saw a black leg protruding somewhat from under one of the twin beds. Mrs. Goddard was tying a string to a curtain with her back turned. The maid hurriedly said "I don't believe I fastened that back parlor shutter." My aunt quickly replied, " Oh, go and see," and the maid rushed to the back of the house and whispered to the cook there was a man under Mrs. Goddard's bed and then down she flew and over the fence to the next neighbours who called the police, but by the time the six policemen arrived to search the house, the man had crawled out and my aunt hearing the rustle thought it was a bat of which she had a deadly fear. The man pointed a pistol at her and said, "If you make any noise I will shoot you." The dear little slender body rose in indignation and said "Then you will walk, sir," which he did immediately and finding his way to the lighted cook's room said, "I want to get out of this house and I want you to show me the way," which she very politely did and when he passed out the front door she closed it on him saying, "Thank you, sir." This was a great story for months after about dear little Mrs. Goddard who had been looking for a man under her bed for many years. She kept up wonderfully, but after that her maid slept in the twin bed.

One other tragic story with its comic side must be told. A former maid named Margaret had taken her usual Thursday afternoon off expecting to return at 10 P. M. She did not come and they waited up half the night. My sister was a guest at that time and the next day at 10 A. M., a telegram came from the maid's brother. "You will never again see Margaret Jane. She was killed by a train." After the shock of the first few days, we were told of the tragic and polite message.

It did not seem fitting that little timid frail woman should have such shocks, but she bore all the ills that came to her with a quiet dignity and survived her generation.

When she passed away at an extreme age, and I took a last look at the little lady in her casket in the old fashioned black gown and dainty white cap, I was surprised at her beautiful face, looking so young and peaceful. And of all the faces I have taken leave of before they were taken to their resting place the one that seemed to shine with an unearthly beauty was that of my Philadelphia aunt.

CHARLOTTE ELIZABETH PAGE
At Eighteen

CHAPTER XII.

REV. CHARLES H. EWING.

CHARLES HENRY EWING, the youngest of his three sisters and a brother, Horace Redman, who died in childhood, was the only grandchild of Dr. John Ewing, who followed his vocation and became a Presbyterian Clergyman. He was only seven when his gifted father died but he never forgot him and I was always conscious of an unusual feeling whenever he spoke of him. He used to tell me how he would carry him in his arms to Belmont to visit Judge Peters, and he always spoke of those trips with his father with emotion. Belmont must have been a delightful Mansion in those days looking down upon the historic city from its hill top and I can imagine the interesting guests that were entertained there. Among them

"the cultured few
By Delaware's green banks I knew,"

which Tom Moore writes of to his friend in England.

My father was named after that son of James Wilson, whose early death was such a grief to my grandmother, who had grown up with him more as a sister than a cousin and named three of her children after those beloved cousins. Mary Wilson writes to her friend, Miss Chauncey, in New Haven, she thinks her brothers Bird and Charles are very extraordinary men and in another letter she speaks of Charles' admiration for his little Redman Cousins.

My father preached much in the South, at first Alexandria

and Baltimore and then in Geneva, New York, where his son and oldest child was born. It was when he was preaching in the South he met my Mother, Charlotte Elizabeth Page, daughter of Captain Jery Lee Page, of Fairfax County, Virginia, a cousin of General Robert E. Lee.

Perhaps it was from Captain Page he acquired such a love for the sea and ships and he took such an interest in the sailors and when he came back to the city of his birth and ancestors he took charge of the Mariner's Bethel and was untiring in his efforts for

"the men who went down to the sea in ships."

It was always said of him, he preached like a lawyer but instead of a Blackstone it was the Bible.

The church magazine said of him, "He was a man who gave very careful preparation to his sermons and was eminently a biblical preacher setting forth the truths he found in his constant study of the Word of God." The Press said, "He was all his life a great Bible student and as a speaker he was forceable and impressive and in his younger day was regarded as one of the most successful revivalists who labored in the South." Coming out of church one morning as a child I remember hearing a man say, "That minister gives you the Bible from Genesis to Revelations and can tell you where any text is to be found." No doubt this lawyer-like manner he inherited from his father and the scientific analysis from his Grandfather.

I enjoyed hearing my mother tell of the first meeting with my father. She was visiting her sister Lucy, who had married Dr. D. H. Emerson, a relative of Ralph Waldo Emerson and son of Dr. Emerson of Christ Church, Salem, Mass., who was the pastor of my grandparents. One morning she came down to breakfast and announced she had seen her future husband in a dream. This delighted my aunt for

Charlotte was the youngest and the beauty of the family but so far had shown no interest in any of her numerous admirers, and in that day girls were soon called old maids, which was not a pleasant opprobrium. Mr. Ewing was expected to come and preach for Dr. Emerson several weeks. When he arrived and was introduced to my mother she recognized him as the man of her dream. In three weeks they were engaged. The following letter written by her sister Ellen, who had married the Hon. Horace Upton, who afterwards became United States Consul to Switzerland (and lived with his family in Geneva for many years), was written to Mrs. Emerson just after the engagement was announced:

"ELLENDALE, Friday,
"June 10th, 1844.

"MY BELOVED SISTER:—

"You ask in your letter to Charlotte why Ellen does not write to you. My excuse is the same as yours, so much to do. I suppose you know we have swarmed again from the old hive and commenced work in a new one. I came here the 12th of April, a few days after Charlotte returned home.

"Horace was in Washington and I moved here alone and I have been alone ever since for the girls have been so much engaged with company at home that I have hardly seen them. Our home is in the heart of the forest not far distant from the turnpike but surrounded by a thick woods, with a boy and girl in the kitchen.

"I stay here night after night frightened out of my wits; how would you like it?

"Horace comes out always on Saturday and has been out two or three times in the week since I came here, but the session of Congress is drawing to a close and he can't leave now but once a week.

"I must stop writing about myself and talk of the new members of the family.

Firstly, Mr. Ewing. I was so afraid I should be disappointed in him, for I had formed a husband for Charlotte out of my own imagination, but I was not in the least. I think him one of the loveliest men I ever knew. I admired his manners, I admire his face, I admire his talents and his whole character so far as I know it, and I think he will make Lotty perfectly happy. Could I say more? Tell me do you like him as well as we do, yes, I know you must. C. is very happy with him, and perfectly devoted and he must think she is "Gould" by the way he looks at her. Pa is delighted with him and all the family love him already and will be sorry to have him leave.

"Of course you know that Charles is engaged to Miss Priscilla Webster, of Washington. She is a native of Augusta, Maine, and came from there three years ago and resides with a sister in W., Mrs. De Lindsly. They are cousins of Dan'l Webster, and very intimate in his family, which of course does not raise them in my estimation. Priscy has been staying with Ma for two weeks and they are all delighted with her. She is very domestic, takes the whole care of her sister's baby and can make all sorts of good things. *Aren't you glad though?* I suppose you would like to know what she looks like. She is very pretty, called handsome, much taller than Charles, round face, beautiful complexion, pretty brown hair and blue eyes with long dark eyelashes, did not notice how often she winked, but I think I have been quite particular enough in my description; of course you are much obliged to me for the sketch of sister *Priscy* (so called), O, I forgot one item, they will be married next fall. Mr. Ewing has been preaching in Washington two weeks every night (I believe) and for the two last Sundays in Alexandria: he is very popular, I am told. Ma went to A. with him and was perfectly charmed, and Horace was very much pleased with him as a preacher.

"What shall I say to my old friend and schoolmate Susan? Tell her I would give anything I possess to have her here this minute, she does not want to see me more than I want to see her. I would go back with her to *old time*s and we, would be girls together again.

"Give my best and warmest love to her, and beg her to come and see me, for I do not look forward to the time when I shall leave home, and I never expect to see Salem again.

"I was sadly disappointed because I could not come to C. and often think of it with tears in my eyes for I am so impatient to see you all, but you must not fail to come here this summer and Mr. Emerson with you. I long to see your children. Alfred is such a driving character he would be first rate among the *Niggers* wouldn't he?

(This son Alfred Emerson became a Navy Officer but died some years ago.)

"Pageville has been quite gay this season. Harriet Howard is still there, and never a day passes without visitors.

"I should be distracted if I had to entertain so much company, but Ma does not mind it, is always prepared and makes every one happy and comfortable, Ah, me, I wish I was like her in many things. Rebecca is at Pageville and I miss her very much for she is such a woman, she is excellent company for me. I wish you could see Helen now, she is thought beautiful by all and I must think so too, I am afraid she will lose some of her beauty before you come if you do not make haste; children change so much in a short time. Lucy is very pretty and a very sweet child, quite a belle among gentlemen. I have a very pretty and snug cottage. If Horace was here I should be quite happy but without him, I do not enjoy anything, he is quite as anxious to be here as I am to have him and we are both looking forward with joy to the 17th of this month which is the day Congress adjourns.

"I don't know that I have written you anything new in this letter for I don't know who of the family may have written to you, as I have not seen them this week. Charlotte and Harriet Howard are on a visit to Miss Webster and will return home to-morrow.

"Give my best love to Hopkins and tell him to come here *quick*. I consider myself quite fortunate to have had such amiable ministers for brothers. Horace says, 'Charlotte did not take a crooked stick after all.'

"Don't put off your visit until cool weather, but come now and stay until it is cool enough to go home.

"Bring your biggest jug and I'll give you more peach marmalade to carry home than I did last time. Do write soon.

"Ever your affectionate Sis

"ELLEN.

"Helen wears all the little dresses you sent without any alterations. I have not bought anything new for her, and I am very much obliged to you dear sister, I take pleasure in using them and always think of sweet little Lucy when I look at them, she is wearing more beautiful garments now.

"I was at Mama's yesterday. All well. Mr. Ewing preached in Alexandria; Charlotte was there with him. They return to Pageville to-day. Mr. E. will be there this week."

My grandfather's plantation was eight miles from Washington in Fairfax County, and when our Aunt Emerson would come to visit us, we loved nothing better than to hear her talk over their young days, and the Pageville gaieties. She had a fund of stories that were never exhausted and five minutes after she arrived the whole house would be laughing. She radiated sunshine and good cheer and her faith and trust in her Heavenly Father was absolute.

After her joyous girlhood she had the usual trials and tribulations of bringing up a large family on the meager salary of many clergymen of her day. At one time in three years there were six deaths in her home and only once was her spirit crushed, when her youngest and most gifted son had taken charge of his first church and almost immediately broke down and was brought home to die.

She survived them all but she was never quite the same after this unexpected sorrow.

She often told us of the Divinity School that was very near Pageville and how the students would find their way to the hospitable Southern home. My grandfather threatened to put up a sign on the gates "Students Retreat." One day one of them who was much enamoured of my mother overstayed his time and hurriedly retraced his steps as it was his turn to take charge of the evening service. He quickly handed his hymn book to a student who was near and whispered "Find me a hymn." His fellow student knew very well where he had been and handed the open hymn book when he was ready to read it out to the audience. The following lines created no little amusement:—

> O may these Heavenly Pages be
> My ever dear delight,
> And still new beauties may I see
> And find increasing light.

I loved to hear my Aunt tell of the dinner parties at Pageville when the noted men of the day would ride out from Washington.

Daniel Webster whose relative married their brother, Henry Clay and General Robert E. Lee, whom they all adored and my mother was so excited at her first dinner party, she upset her champagne. If Dr. Johnson had attended some of those dinner parties in Old Virginia, he no doubt would have changed his opinion of the "Plantations" as he called America.

Mrs. Emerson enjoyed telling amusing stories even if the laugh was on herself and at one time when money was scarce with many mouths to feed for her home was always open to any members of the family, with true Southern hospitality. She was wearing a bonnet that had become very shabby and one of the wealthy members of the congregation noticing it begged that she might send her a new one.

On the evening of the day it arrived, Mrs. Emerson tried it on and did not feel it was quite suited to her head. She was a little thin woman with no pretension to beauty as I remember her in her middle and old age, but one never thought of that. Her soul and her mind overshadowing the physical. Coming down stairs to go to service with her married daughter the latter said, "O, Ma, that bonnet is impossible. Where is that new one that was sent you?" So to please her daughter she went back to her room and put on the new one and came down joining her daughter outside where she was waiting in the dark.

When she followed her little mother up the Church aisle she was horrified to see this monstrous thing perched on top of her head, but she kept her horror to herself not wishing to disturb the sweet serenity of the little plain face that was under it. The next morning however, that bonnet was ripped apart and they retrimmed the headgear for the family out of it.

Mrs. JERY LEE PAGE

My aunt always declared there was at least a peck of trimming on it and she never ceased to laugh at the memory of herself walking up that Church aisle and her daughter's consternation.

Ellen Page had a very different life from her sister. I only knew her by the charming letters she wrote to my mother from Geneva, filled with interesting details of her life in Europe.

Several little clippings have come down to me regarding my Uncle Horace Upton, written by his friend Col. Forney of the "Philadelphia Press." While on a visit to Geneva, in 1867, he sent home a long article, descriptive of that city and ends it with a tribute to the U. S. Consul and his family:—

"I cannot close this letter without a tribute to a faithful public servant, Horace Upton, Esq., the American Consul to Geneva. I was prepared from the reports of others, to find the same courteous and patriotic gentleman, I had known in Washington at the outbreak of the rebellion, when his fine estate at Upton's Hill was desolated by the contending armies, and especially by the traitors, who never forgave his early and continued devotion to his country, but it was only when I saw for myself his attention to the interests of Americans and to his public duties, which are neither light nor always agreeable that I understood the full value of such a man in such a post. Poorly paid and constrained to cultivate the utmost economy, his refined family is the result of our educated country people, and his benevolent efforts are always ready to assist the distressed. In saying this much, I feel I am doing simple justice to an honest, modest, and thorough-bred gentleman, and repeating the opinion of all American travelers."

J. W. FORNEY.

The following eulogy was written for the Press also after Mr. Upton's death:—

"The Hon. Charles Horace Upton, U. S. Chargé d'Affaires in Switzerland, who died a few days since, is thus spoken of in the 'Philadelphia Press' by a gentleman who knew him long and well.

"He was a man of vast knowledge both of human nature and human works. He was a scholarly man and a student. I well remember calling on him one morning, when not finding him at home I waited his return. Pretty soon he came in, his face all aglow. 'Well,' he said, 'I have been to the library to look up a latin quotation. I knew I was right and I am. Here it is.' He was full of wit and humor and a courtly gentleman. His hospitality unbounded and aided by his wife the Consulate was made a home to Americans abroad. One trait in his character is especially to be noticed. He was a charitable man; he never spoke ill of any one, always endeavoring to speak of the good rather than the bad points in the character of his acquaintances. He was generous to a fault, with a heart and hand ever open to the voice of distress. In his official duties he was exact, honorable and courteous and universally respected and beloved."

The Uptons had several daughters. Lucy was not only a great beauty but a remarkable character.

I never saw her but once when she came to bid my mother good-bye before sailing to join her parents in Geneva. I was only a little child but I was impressed and awed by her beauty and her radiant personality which seemed to envelope the entire room where she sat in the center with a large white hat encircled by a black ostrich feather which fell gracefully down one side some what in the style of today but such style and distinction of manner, I regret we seldom see today. Many letters were written to my mother

LUCY UPTON
Mrs. Pericles Lazaro

from her parents telling of the attention she received from noted people in Geneva.

She married the Greek Consul to Saloniki, Pericles Lazaro. She did not long survive the birth of her little son Cleon. She was so beloved on the day of her funeral the shops were closed and many mourned her early death.

Years after her husband came to America and paid his respects to my mother who had been so beloved by his adored wife. He was tall and slender and very handsome, but his face was grave and sad and the tears came to his eyes when he spoke of my beautiful Cousin Lucy. Their little boy was the pride of his grandmother's heart. When he was five she wrote us he could speak five languages and when a very young man and we were both visiting my sister in Washington, who had married into the Diplomatic Corps, we found him a very delightful cultured result of German and French Universities, although not quite out of his teens.

Estelle Upton was always delicate and did not long survive her sister. One story has come down to me.

When Longfellow visited the Uptons in Geneva, he was much pleased to find my cousin had set several of his poems to music and entertained him one evening by singing them to him.

The following morning he asked her to take a stroll with him to the famous book shops in that city. In one he asked the bookseller what he would consider the best and finest English book to give as a present. We can understand his surprise and pleasure when the man handed him a copy of his own poems and Cousin Estelle astonished the man by telling him the buyer was no less a person than Mr. Longfellow himself.

CHAPTER XIII.

DR. CHARLES GRAFTON PAGE.

DR. CHARLES GRAFTON PAGE, my mother's brother, was for years Examiner of Patents and himself well known in scientific circles as an inventor. His most famous invention was the Ruhmkorff Coil, part of the Atlantic cable. As an officer of the Patent Office he could never receive awards. But after his death a Frenchman pirated his invention and received 100,000 francs. Then our government waived their customary rule applying to patent officers and awarded the full amount with years' interest to his widow. She was from Augusta, Maine. Priscilla Sewall Webster connected with many prominent New England families, the Codys, Lowells, etc. Her older sisters married Washington men whom they met while visiting their uncle, Dr. Thomas Sewall, of that city. When she was eighteen she came to live with a sister who had married Dr. Lindsly, and three years after married my uncle, Dr. Page. She has written a very charming book for her grandchildren called "Personal Reminiscences." It is full of interesting events of her early years in New England and her experiences in the Capital during long years.

One of her sisters married Dr. Peter Parker, who spent many years in China. He established the Ophthalmic Hospital in Canton in 1835, was sent as Minister from the United States in 1855. One of her cousins and girlhood friends was Louise Weston, who afterwards became a member of the Brook Farm Circle. She was also related to the Choates, and writes of her visits to the home of the

Hon. Rufus Choate, whose sister was the wife of her uncle, Dr. Thomas Sewall. Among the friends and kindred who welcomed her to Washington she writes that none took her more lovingly to their hearts than her noble kinsman, Daniel Webster, and his wife and children, and she delighted in his wonderful intellect, his noble bearing and the indescribable charm of his manner and presence, and many of her happiest days were spent in his family.

A few days after her arrival at Mrs. Lindsly's the inauguration of Harrison took place, and their parlors were filled with guests for the occasion. A Whig President had come in after twelve years of Democratic rule, and Mr. Webster was to be Premier. General Harrison, though born in Virginia, was a Western man and lived in a log cabin during the early days. To add to the enthusiasm of the common people a log cabin was made the emblem of the party. A grand public dinner was given to the incoming President and the distinguished representatives of the Whig party. Art and skill combined to render this dinner magnificent, and among the decorations a log cabin of rock candy standing upon a base of nougat beautifully ornamented with railings of white and colored candy. This, with a small American flag floating from its top, stood near Mr. Webster, and when the dinner was over he said to the gentlemen present: "With the consent of the distinguished guests I would like to send this cabin to a young friend of mine. Every one expressing approval, it was sent to little Webster (Lindsly) and stood upon a table in the parlor.

One month later the funeral of the President took place. The log cabin draped in black still stood upon the table.

Later on my Aunt Priscy writes of the elegant dinner given by the Websters to Lord Ashburton, to the President and Cabinet, and foreign Ministers to which she was sometimes invited and not infrequently being the only lady present, except Mrs. Webster, the seat of honor would be given her by Mr. Webster's side . She says: "He never enjoyed the grand dinners as much as the cosy little ones he used to get up for particular friends and which were prepared by his own invaluable cook, Monachy. He always went to market before breakfast and would seek the first early spring blossoms from the country people and take great pride in having bouquets by the side of our plates when we came to breakfast." This was after his son Fletcher and his family had left and she spent a good deal of time with Mrs. Webster.

She writes of her first New Year's calls at the White House, on Mrs. Madison, whose receptions were always very elegant, also upon Mrs. John Quincy Adams, and of her meeting with Mr. Fillmore, President, a few years later. All this reminds me of my visits to Washington as a girl and New Year's Day at the White House during the Harrison and Cleveland administrations when visiting my sister whose husband was a Foreign Minister. We were ushered in by the private entrance for the Diplomatic Corps and passed in first to shake hands with the President, his wife and Cabinet members and then moved just back of them and watched the gay crowd pass in and on to the larger rooms beyond.

Mrs. Cleveland was always so gracious and handsome, and Mrs. Harrison charmed me with her dignity and sweetness—never shaking hands but holding a beautiful bouquet and smiling at you so kindly. I always thought her not shaking hands was a great relief from this American custom which is so fatiguing and unnecessary.

To return to Miss Webster, at this time she met Mrs. Commodore Stewart, whose beautiful daughter Delia married Mr. Parnell, and their little son became the Irish Patriot whose rash zeal reminded her so much of her old friend, his very interesting grandmother, who loved to talk to her of her little grandson who became so famous in later years. Her sister, Mrs. Lindsly, about this time invited my uncle to a social evening where he delighted them all with his music.

Miss Webster says she admired him greatly and thought him far more interesting and finer looking than any of the gentlemen who were attentive to her. Soon they were engaged and she wrote to her cousin and received the following reply:—

"BOSTON, August 1, 1844.

"MY DEARLY BELOVED PRISCY:—

"I received your affectionate letter two or three days ago, and read it with deep emotion. Your former letter to Mrs. W. had communicated to us your choice of a husband, an event so important to the happiness of your life. I cannot say I was sorry; on the contrary I know I ought to be glad, as I believe your choice an exceedingly good one; but then I could not help feeling that your marriage would draw you away in some measure by other ties, and that hereafter you must belong principally, not to former friends and connections, but to another. I have not much personal acquaintance, my dear cousin, with Dr. Page, but have ever received an excellent character of him. He is a friend, I believe, of Fletcher's, and I know much of him, also, through Mr. Elsworth and others. You cannot doubt that I think him a most fortunate man, and my blessing and all my good wishes attend you both. May God protect your lives and health and make your union happy.

"I shall be in Washington in this month or the next, and

shall be most happy to become better acquainted with Dr. Page. You yourself will ever be to me an object of tender regard and affection, and it will be a sincere pleasure to see you prosperous and happy. When you write your sister give her my best love and regards. I go to New York today to be gone a week on professional business.

"I pray you make my respects and my felicitations to Dr. Page, and my regards to Dr. Lindsly.

"Yours ever affectionately,

"DAN'L. WEBSTER.

"To Miss P. S. Webster.

"Mrs. Webster has written you, she is now at Marshfield."

Forty years after, Mrs. Page writes for her grandchildren that her new parents and sisters gave her as warm a welcome as was awarded by her uncle, brothers, sisters and cousins to their dear grandfather who on that evening became a part of her life and continued her most beloved companion and friend for nearly twenty-four years, when she was left without his strong arm to lean on. The day after their wedding they started for Boston, where many of Dr. Page's relations lived, and they were delightfully entertained. She found my uncle a great favorite among them all. Then they spent several days at Marshfield. Mr. Webster was obliged to be absent, but his wife was always a delightful hostess and their daughter Julia (Mrs. Appleton) was at home and Caroline, her eldest child, became Madame Bonaparte and lived near the Pages in Washington.

The autumn days at Marshfield were delightful, only she regretted the absence of the great statesman who had promised to tell her the history of the Websters. She adds many years after he had passed away she again visited the old mansion, but there was no one to tell her of her ancestors and show her the family tree. A year later the house was burned and with it perished many of the relics of the past.

In one chapter my Aunt Priscy describes their little dinner parties and breakfasts which Daniel Webster particularly enjoyed. She says it was a great treat also to have him and Mr. Choate together for an evening. Their brilliant wit and ready repartee afforded them all immense amusement, and she adds: "The charm of society as it then existed in Washington can, I am sure, never be repeated." As the French say, *je me demande*. I can remember in my girlhood at my sister's delightful dinners, every guest at the table was a celebrated person in this country and from over seas—statesmen, diplomats, social celebrities, authors, and world famous portrait painters, etc., etc. No social life in this country can be compared to that of Washington.

The Pages of Salem and Virginia.

John Ewing's grandson, Charles Henry Ewing, had the same admiration for his wife's parents as their daughter-in-law, who took them to her home after all their children were married and their plantation in Fairfax County was sold. Mrs. Page's mother, Mrs. Webster, also lived with them and they seem to have been a most harmonious group. She writes that it was her privilege to have them with her. Of Captain Page she says: "He was a handsome, gallant gentleman of the old school who would not have allowed a lady to stoop for her handkerchief or fan even at the age of eighty-four. He never neglected to present his wife with a bouquet of fresh flowers each day, which she wore in her dress, and very lovely she looked with her lace handkerchief folded over her breast, her pretty brown curls and sweet, sympathetic blue eyes seated in her camp chair which Captain Page would take out into the grove on warm afternoons while he sat by her side and read aloud, or talked upon subjects interesting to them both."

When Captain Page's father went to live in Salem, Mass., he married Lois Lee, daughter of Captain Richard Lee, and they lived in the house which was afterwards occupied by Judge Endicott, of Salem—a fine mansion in those days, with handsome carved wood in the finishing. My Great-grandfather Page, she says, was luxurious in his tastes, and extravagantly fond of music, which my grandfather and her husband, Dr. Page, showed the same talent for. They all played upon several instruments, and my great-grandfather would have musicians stationed in the hall to play while he dined. This gave rise to a saying among the common people that "Mr. Page was such a grand gentleman he had to have his victuals played down his throat." My lovely and beloved grandmother was a Salem girl of that famous Derby family whose ancestor was Roger Derby, and the name Lucy has come down to the writer from a Lucy Derby said to be remarkable for beauty and accomplishments. She came over from England in the early days of the Massachusetts colony, and they say she was so overcome with grief at the death of her husband she fell dead upon his grave. It was a cousin of my great-grandmother Derby, John Derby, who carried the first news of the war to England and raced his vessel across the Atlantic (as fast as one could race in those days) in order to give his version of the affair. When asked his price he put it down a cipher. Elias Haskett Derby, another cousin, built his stately mansion on Derby Square, but when he died no one had quite money enough to keep it up, so it was pulled down and much of it today adorns other buildings in Salem. Derby Square is now the Market Square, but Derby wharf and Derby Street and New Derby Street serve to remind the City of Salem of one of its most important families of

DERBY MANSION ON DERBY SQUARE, SALEM, MASS.

Colonial days. My Great-grandmother Derby married William Lang, of Salem, and my Grandmother Page writes to her daughter-in-law in Washington of the reunion of nine daughters in the old home which is still occupied by their descendants.

Dr. Emerson, her old pastor, presided at the reunion, and the youngest of the sisters prepared the elegant dinner. It was her daughter who married Bishop Clarke, of Rhode Island, and Rev. D. H. Emerson, the son of the pastor, married my aunt, Lucy Page, my mother's oldest sister, and the delight of our home when it was her pleasure to grace it. I was a very small child when our grandparents came to visit us in Philadelphia, but I was impressed with their loveliness of character and serenity. From her picture, which hangs on my wall and charms every one who looks at it, I can well imagine how she looked as a younger woman, and the following acrostic has come down to me, discovered among my mother's papers. I do not know who wrote it, but of one thing I am sure it did not exaggerate:—

ACROSTIC TO LUCY LANG PAGE.

Lovely as the new blown rose,
 Unhurt by evening dew,
Charming in its angel power,
 Youth's bosom ever new

Long may such loveliness increase
 And adorn each genial mind,
No rose that opens to the morn
 Gives beauty so divine.

After living several years with their son, Dr. Page, they spent their last years with their daughter, Mrs. Emerson, in St. George's, Delaware, where Dr. Emerson was pastor of a church. On learning of her death the "Salem Register" published the following obituary:—

"Obituary.

"Died in St. George's, Delaware, on the 21st of March, Lucy L. Page, wife of Capt. Jery Lee Page, formerly of Salem, Mass., in the 83rd year of her age.

"Mrs. Page was the fourth daughter of William Lang, Esq., of Salem, and there are many in this city who remember his family of three sons and nine daughters, and who recall with admiration the many virtues of the family. Mrs. Page left Salem with her husband about thirty years ago and lived for twenty-five years in Fairfax County, Va. About five years since she left Virginia and resided with her husband in Washington, D. C., and thence she came to the house of her son-in-law, Rev. D. H. Emerson, in St. George's, Delaware, where after blessing his family by her delightful piety two years, she peacefully passed from the earth and entered into the joy of her Lord. Being a member of the Old South Church in Salem, she associated herself with the wife of the pastor in all the benevolent operations of the day and was distinguished by her zeal in the labors of the Moral Society, in the efforts of the Maternal Association, in the cause of educating young men for the ministry and in the attempts then making for the elevation of seamen and for the bestowal of pecuniary aid upon seamen's widows and orphan children. Many were the sailor's wives who received her bounty and many were the orphans of poor sailors who arose to call her blessed.

"While living in Virginia she carried out the same zeal for doing good and by her benefactions, always sustained by her husband, towards schools and churches and especially towards the Theological Seminary of the Episcopal Church in her neighborhood. She changed the aspect of that part of Virginia and made its desolations bud and blossom as the rose. She established the first Sabbath School for colored children that was ever known in that part of Virginia, and she regularly taught in that school until it was broken up by the police.

"While residing in Washington she still seemed to live for the purpose of doing good, and many were the poor refugees from Virginia and the sick and wounded soldiers who were aided from the stores of her bounty. She was daily employed in preparing clothing, cordials and medicines for the sick soldiers in the hospitals, and for such her prayers and advice and money were freely given.

"When Mrs. Page came to Delaware, being then 80 years of age, one would have said she was now entitled to perfect rest, but still she found her sweetest rest in doing good. Her conversations on faith, on prayer, on perfect submission to the will of God, to the love of Jesus and on Heaven were blessed to those who heard them, and many of the ladies of the congregation formed for her an exalted Christian friendship. Her example too was Heavenly, for she was never known to murmur or complain, but in all her trials, she regarded everything as ordered by the will of the Blessed Redeemer, and as exactly right, etc., etc."

This article was written for the "Salem Register" by her son-in-law, Rev. D. H. Emerson, at whose home she spent her last days. He was a son of Dr. Emerson, of Old South Church, Salem, and her pastor in early life before she removed to Virginia.

If I should write a chapter on the beauty of face and character of Charlotte Elizabeth Page, who married Rev. Chas. Henry Ewing, I fear my readers would agree with the lady who said to me once: "O, yes, nearly all mothers are beautiful and lovely to their children," so I shall only quote the following poems which were found in her little box of laces with the odor of Attar of Rose about them. Her family will all agree the poems do not exaggerate:—

ACROSTIC.

Could I from bright Castalin's fountain sip
Her purest draught to lave a burning lip,
Ah! how would my lyre wak'd by Love's minstrelsy
Respire its wildest, sweetest strain for thee.
Lov'd one! what charms, the bright, the soft, the sweet,
Of radiant beauty in thy aspect meet.
The fairy form—the artless winning grace,
The soul that breathes in music from the face.
Earth has no gem whose ray serenely bright,
E'er matched that eye's soft beam of azure light;
Lo! o'er that brow imperial throne of thought
(Its classic mould in Parian marble wrought)
Zenobia paints her palist languores there,
And throws in ringlets wild her raven hair;
But lovelier far that *Mind* whose light like rays
Electric o'er thy features wildly plays
This the bright charm, when Beauty's fading flower
Has droop'd and wither'd in her radiant bower.
Pure, gentle, mild as that first vestal ray
Aurora sheds to gild the opening day.
Gem of Beauty! starry Bird of Heaven,
Each spell to charm the heart to thee is given.

"Zenobia, Queen of Palmyra, was celebrated for her great beauty. She was taken captive and led in chains to Rome by Aurelian. While in this condition she is painted by Titian with luxuriant hair falling over a brow of the most exquisite whiteness."

E. W. H.

Pass thou on for the vow is said
   That is never broken;
The hand of blessing hath trembling laid
On thy young and guileless head
   And the word is spoken
By lips that never their words betrayed.

Pass thou on for thy human all
   Is richly given,
And the voice that claimed its holy thrall
Must be sweeter for life than music's fall,
   And this side heaven
Thy lips may never that trust recall.

Pass thou on! yet many an eye
   Will droop and glisten,
And the trusting heart in vain will try
To still its pulse as thy step goes by
   And we vainly listen
For thy voice of witching melody.

Pass on! There is not of our blessings one
   That may not perish.
Like visiting angels whose errand is done,
They are never at rest 'till their home is won,
   And we may not cherish
The beautiful gift of thy light. Pass on!